NAPA WINE COUNTRY

NAPA WINE COUNTRY

PHOTOGRAPHY AND TEXT
BY EARL ROBERGE

International Standard Book Number 0-912856-22-X
Library of Congress Catalog Number 75-16054
Copyright© 1975 by Publisher • Charles H. Belding
Graphic Arts Center Publishing Company
2000 N. W. Wilson • Portland, Oregon 97209 • 503/224-7777
Designer • Robert Reynolds
Printer • Graphic Arts Center
Bindery • Lincoln & Allen
Printed in the United States of America

To Joe Heitz, superb winemaker,
gracious and generous host,
secret intellectual, good friend,
and to Alice, his good right arm,
this book is affectionately dedicated.

CONTENTS

"This is the story

of a place   ix

. . . . . its people.

. . . . . . its product

. . . . . . its way

of life.

A Land Created on a Day

when God was Smiling

It is called

the Napa Valley.

whom I can't possibly thank enough. This is one of the bonuses my stay in the Valley has produced. Bob and Patsy will hopefully be my friends for the rest of my life.

A stay of several months, with a dinner invitation almost every night would produce a very long list of "Thank You's" so here I must hedge a bit and start expressing my appreciation in general, rather than specifically. My Chapter XII, "La Dolce Vita" was personally researched . . . and thoroughly! There are highlights, of course: the baronial splendor and easy warmth of Elizabeth and Louis Martini's beautiful home, the wonderful music, banter and repartee around Margrit and Phil Biever's table, the easy informality, good food and fine wine found at the Tom Lynch and Bill Stafford homes, and the candlelit elegance of Ron and Pat Amick's lovely Rutherford dining room. My thanks also go to Peter Mondavi, for his gracious hospitality. Then, too, who could ever forget that lovely dinner at the Hanns Kornell ranch, where over a hundred people were entertained effortlessly and gracefully by a host and hostess to whom a tour de force like this seems to come easily? My special thanks also go to Johnsye Dietz who dresses up any table not only with her spectacular good looks, but also with superlative music, conversation and cookery.

Many of the outstanding vintners in the Napa Valley got their start somewhere else. Donn and Molly Chappellet are people who left a millionaire socialite existence in Beverly Hills for the much more rewarding experience of living on Pritchard Hill and making good wine. To Donn, Molly and all the children, my thanks for having taken me into your family circle and making me feel at home. The several times I have sat at your table and taken in some of the best the Napa Valley can afford, whether it be food, wine, conversation, scenery or beauty, rank as some of the most enjoyable events in a year studded with memorable moments.

The Napa Valley has often been accused of not sufficiently tooting its own horn, but I met a few people who do a pretty good job of telling the world about what a wonderful place it is. Margot Venezia, of Oakville Vineyards, Bob Pecota, of Beringer Bros., Joe Maganini of Charles Krug, Maynard Moynihan of Beaulieu, Jerry Gleeson of the Christian Brothers, and Brady McManus of Inglenook all are competent people who have my admiration for the work they do, and my thanks for the help they have given me. Then, there's Margrit Biever.

Margrit is one of those phenomena that occur only too seldom. Long before I had the pleasure of meeting her, I had heard of Margrit, and found myself wondering whether it could be possibly true that one woman could conduct V.I.P. tours in eight languages, arrange a concert, translate technical letters into four languages, cook a superb dinner for thirty people, run a very efficient public relations department, and be at all times one of the most consummate charmers anyone could ever observe, and all in the course of one day's work! She can, and does do all these things, and with a flair that makes her the envy of anyone who tries to emulate her. She also plays a smashing game of tennis and is, at all times, a completely delightful person to know. My thanks, admiration and affection to you, Margrit, for the unstinted help you have given me in putting together this book. It just wouldn't have been nearly as much fun without you. My thanks also to Norma

Fuchs, Margrit's efficient secretary who always had a kind word and good solid advice.

To David Heitz, Mike Stone, Joe Phelps, Tom Burgess, Jim Nichelini, Keith and Marian Bowers, Margo Venezia, Bill and Barbara Lincoln, Charles Wagner, Jerry Draper, Chuck Carpy, Larry Solari, Mike and Mary Ellen Golick and to the many, many people who took me by the hand and showed me the splendors of the Napa Valley, my sincere and heartful thanks.

Most writers and photographers would gladly give up six months of their lives to have as good an editor and publisher as I have in Charles H. Belding. I didn't even have to do that! In fact, I honestly believe that the very satisfactory meeting of the minds we have achieved has materially lengthened our life spans, as well as enriching our respective lives. Here is a man dedicated to quality and hard work: virtues that help not a little in producing a fine book. To Charles, and to all the dedicated craftsmen and members of the Graphic Arts family who from the very start had confidence in this book, my thanks and appreciation.

I have intentionally saved till last my expressions of appreciation to Joe and Alice Heitz, and to my wife, Gertie, for without their help, this book would still be an unfulfilled dream. Joe and Alice gave me not only their unqualified help, but also their friendship. Their delightful little guest house ("Tobacco Road West," I believe a former occupant had named it), became for me "the Heitz Hilton" and sheltered me for a total of well over two months. It was not only shelter, but also a place where I knew there would be good food, companionship, and wine such as few people are ever privileged to drink. But mostly, it was a place where I knew I could be with friends.

Right from the very beginning, Joe and Alice have given this project their unstinting help and enthusiasm. Around the Heitz table I have met people from all over the world, and tasted superb wines poured with a lavish hand, for no one drinks better wine than Joe Heitz, unless it is his guests. It is only fitting and proper that this book should be dedicated to Joe and Alice, for no one has helped more in its making. But, then, these are my friends. To them, helping anyone is second nature, but helping a friend is a primary impulse.

The most difficult part of writing, I am told, is to express in words feelings that are so deep and basic that words somehow seem painfully inadequate; and so it is when I try to say "Thank You" to my wife, Gertie. Throughout the making of this book, she has been my rock of refuge. She has helped, encouraged, bolstered and solaced me with the suggestions and gentle understanding that only a good wife who is your other half can provide.

For the many hours spent at a typewriter trying to decipher my sometimes frenetic scrawl, for lawns laboriously mowed in my absence, for the many precious days and nights we could have had together, but didn't, because this book had to be done, for all the wonderful things you are . . .

I don't have to say it, because you know, as always, what is in my heart.

Earl Roberge ASMP

Walla Walla, Washington

INTRODUCTION

When Noah looked around, somewhere east of Ararat for the best possible site for his vineyard, he not only started an industry, but also initiated a search that has gone on to this day with unabated vigor. Over the centuries, special places favored with the right combination of soil, climate, moisture and elevation have become highly prized, to the point that many wars have been fought, and much blood shed to secure this possession.

The Bordeaux region of France, the fabled hills of Burgundy, and the terraced slopes of the Rheingau are world famous simply because they have demonstrated over a span of many centuries that they can consistently yield a superior wine, not because of some isolated fortunate accident, but as the predictable result of a happy set of circumstances that are duplicated in only a very few places in the world.

Over a long span of time, a store of facts and legends has collected around these areas. They have become renowned in song and verse as happy lands, where the work is hard and exacting, but also as places where the earth gratefully receives the kiss of the sun, and when lovingly caressed, is generous with her favors.

The history of wine is so interwoven with the history of man that it would be futile to try to separate them. No one knows with any certainty when the first wine was made: more likely than not it was the result of some happy accident. Some prehistoric caveman, on visiting his store of previously harvested grapes probably found that some of them had become crushed, and had released a juice that had miraculously been changed into a liquid that not only was delicious to the taste, but which induced a euphoria previously unknown in a life not particularly noted for creature comforts. Certainly it was known to the ancient Egyptians and Sumerians. The odes of Homer are replete with references to it, and the Phoenicians made it a principal item of commerce. There are 167 references to wine in the Bible—mostly complimentary, for in an area where water was either scarce or contaminated, wine offered a safe, delightful beverage that was very much part of every day life. The Jewish Sabbath observance features wine, and it is no coincidence that when Jesus Christ, at the Last Supper, commanded his disciples to repeat that sacred rite, he chose as its symbols bread and wine, the everyday staples that were the mainstays of life.

The flowering of the Roman Empire gave wine and viticulture a tremendous impetus since the Romans soon found that one of the best ways to stabilize and civilize nomadic tribes was to engage them in raising grapes. The hard labor attendant to the practice of viticulture not only burned off energy otherwise dissipated in warfare, but it also bound the people to one spot. It takes years to successfully propagate a vineyard, and no one is about to leave an endeavor that has occupied a major portion of one's adult life. And so, we see the Roman Emperors settling their veterans in the provinces, granting them riverfront sites, and raising in Cisalpine Gaul and along the Danube vineyards that were to become the most prolific in the Empire.

In 92 A.D., the Emperor Domitian, fearful of the competition of the provincial vineyards over those of Italy, ordered all vineyards in Cisalpine Gaul to be uprooted. The Emperor's edict was honored more in the

Towering over the Northern Valley, Mt. St. Helena is the central theme. Once heavily wooded, it was almost totally denuded by a disastrous forest fire in 1964, but is now once more sprouting its usual coat of evergreens. *Right:* Nestled amidst its leaves of green, crimson and gold, a cluster of Napa Gamay grapes await the hand of the picker. *Pages 24-25:* From the top of the mountains near Angwin, day dyes the fog banks over the Pacific and outlines in orange light, the mountain ridges that border the Napa Valley.

breach than it was in fact, for by this time the local governors were beginning to realize the true worth of the experiment that had primarily been intended to civilize a warlike people. In places under the direct control and supervision of the Emperor, the edict was more or less honored, but in the far-flung reaches of Gaul there were many places where the word from Rome was either ignored, or never received. In 293 A.D. the Emperor Probus, a more pragmatic ruler, donned the imperial purple and the edict was rescinded. The desire for good wine was stronger than official decree, a lesson obviously lost on those who foisted the Prohibition Amendment on the American people.

By this time, a pattern was beginning to emerge. Certain lands raised better grapes than others: some regions raised certain varieties of grapes to a unique degree of excellence, while others were better suited to cereal crops or fruits. Already the Bordeaux region, and Burgundy were being proclaimed the equal or superior to the more established wine lands of Italy or Northern Africa. It took some time for their preeminence to be established, but the process was already under way.

The discoveries of the late Middle Ages and the intellectual ferment induced by the Renaissance also added to the interest in new wine lands. The island of Madeira was discovered, found to be very good wine country, and with the coming of the white man to America, a whole new chapter unfolded.

The first European settlers to the New World brought vine cuttings from their homelands. While the original interests was mainly in producing wine for the celebration of the Mass, it soon became apparent that some areas of the New World were well suited to the grape, and viticulture became one of the main efforts of the missionaries, especially of the indefatigable Franciscans. The vine followed the missions, and in California it found its most fertile ground. The versatile if somewhat plebian Mission grape was planted at most of the missions along the Camino Real and formed the basis for the present wine industry in California.

The measure of any wine producing region is the quality of its product. Measured by this infallible standard, there is one region that should stand as an equal, or even as a superior to the better known wine lands of the world, but like the fabled younger sister in the Cinderella story is still to be fully noticed or appreciated. However, observers with discerning eyes are already predicting that this young land will some day eclipse her older sisters once her beauty has fully matured and is made known to a waiting world.

This is the Napa Valley in North Central California; a land created on a day when God was in a particularly good mood.

The Napa Valley bathes its feet in the salt water of San Pablo Bay, where it is a wide plain. At Carneros, at the southern end, the valley is still mostly flat, with a few hills giving a promise of what is to be. As it marches inland, the valley narrows, the surrounding hills have become small mountains, progressively more densely wooded and soon, at Yountville it has narrowed to a width of only three miles.

The character of the land likewise has been changing, for although Highway 29, which skirts the western edge of the valley is bordered by vineyards almost as soon as it leaves the city limits of Napa, it now is practically

An old, abandoned winery slowly falls apart. Part of an estate which seems incapable of settlement, it is a very desirable property which should be making good wine, as it originally did. *Right:* Early morning on the Yount Mill Road. It is easy to understand why this region had such a hold on George Yount that, with the whole valley at his feet, he chose this part for his home. *Pages 28-29:* Framed in a tangle of azaleas and a flowering plum tree, the Napa Valley slumbers under a blanket of fog, with only the tops of the firs poking through the mist. This scene is from Tom and Linda Burgess' backyard.

surrounded by them. From Yountville to the north the Valley is dedicated wholeheartedly to viticulture. Vineyards are everywhere, filling practically every acre in the valley, and even rising in gentle curves to the slopes of the surrounding mountains.

Along the eastern edge of the valley, from Napa to Calistoga, the Silverado Trail offers some respite from the constant traffic of Highway 29, but its greatest value is in the beautiful vistas it offers of the valley and the western mountains. The original route from the cinnabar mines of Mt. St. Helena to the loading docks on San Pablo Bay, this road once echoed to the rumbling of huge ore wagons and the cracking of the drivers' whips as ponderous oxen slowly dragged huge loads to salt water. Now, it skirts the towns, gently rises over the knolls of the eastern foothills to present one breathtaking vista after another, and is generally a completely satisfying aesthetic experience. Near Yountville, the road skirts the steep mountain promontory known as Stag's Leap, while farther on the scenery becomes more gentle and offers unparalleled vistas of the central and upper valley.

On Highway 29, north of Yountville, there is a large sign, appropriately placed in a vineyard, that tells you that you are now entering the Napa Wine Country. That sign is almost superfluous, for it tells something that is so apparent that its presence is an exercise in redundancy. This is wine country beyond a doubt: that fact washes over one's senses like a living wave. The main business of this valley is grapes and wine; anything else is strictly ancillary. The whole region is so manifestly well suited to the growing of quality wine grapes that denying this fact, or failing to implement it would be tantamount to an act of sacrilege. There is no getting away from it, especially during the time of the crush, when the very air is spicy with the heady odor of fermenting wine, and every breath makes the visitor aware of that fact.

For the next twenty-five miles, the valley runs northward between its sentry guard of mountains, sometimes narrowing to as little as a mile or less then widening out again. At its northern edge it runs point blank into the flanks of Mt. St. Helena, and here it is only about half a mile wide. All along the valley, alluvial fans brought down from the surrounding mountains by the rushing Spring streams spread out, and bring to the soil the variety in composition that has made this the most versatile wine producing region in the United States.

The Napa Valley is actually quite small—easily visited in one day—and would quite handily fit into a corner of the San Joaquin Valley or Bordeaux. It is unquestionably the smallest of the world's major premier wine regions, but its beauty is such that it rightly ranks as one of the world's garden spots. Every year, over a million people pour through it to savor the peculiar charm that the Valley casts so effortlessly. It is a charm enhanced by encircling wooded mountains cradling a verdant land that daily changes its appearance, but is always appealing. It is a wooded land studded with giant oaks, and crisscrossed by tree-shaded lanes. It is a gentle land, where the hand of man has been applied with loving care, so that his ministrations have not scarred the face of Nature, but have usually improved it, and added to an already abundant natural beauty.

In the early Spring, the grape buds come out along with the leaves. Shaped like a miniature cluster of grapes, these buds must expand into flowers and be pollinated before they will grow into a cluster of grapes. *Right:* Renee DeRosa's home in the Carneros region of the Napa Valley fronts on a small lake and is reminiscent of the farmhouses in Normandy. Besides being an avid collector of avant garde art, he also grows some of the best Pinot Noir in the whole Valley.

The Indian name "Napa" means "plenty" and it is indeed a land of plenty, but the Indians themselves called it "Ta-La-Ha-Lu-Si" which freely translates to "Beautiful Land." Even the very first inhabitants seemingly were appreciative of the natural beauty so generously lavished on this region: a beauty which has inspired artists, photographers, poets and writers, and made this valley one of the most sought-after home sites in the world.

It is the story of this beautiful valley that I would like to tell in this book. If I seem a bit fulsome in my praise, please remember that my association with it, as it is with most visitors, has been more in the nature of a love affair than a marriage. One may overlook, or even find endearing faults in a mistress that would be intolerable in a wife, and the Valley is a lovely mistress: seductive, alluring, and promising in her lush beauty all manners of earthly delights. She is also, as those who live here will tell you, a wonderful wife: merry, hard working, bountiful, and forgiving, so that those who have succumbed to her spell gladly spend a lifetime here, and with their dying breath question whether the glories of a promised Paradise hereafter can possibly eclipse those of the one in which they have spent their earthly lives.

Telling the full story of such a place is patently impossible: that would take several lifetimes, nor do I delude myself that I am qualified to do so. All I can do is show and tell of the things I have experienced and observed in my all too short stay in this valley. I make no pretense of being an expert on any phase of life here, only an interested, sympathetic and observant viewer who has experienced a small part of this way of life and found it to be very, very good indeed.

As for the wine scene: that is basic to this valley. Although it is true that there are people living in the Valley who, mostly because of religious convictions, take no part in the manufacture or consumption of the Valley's main product, it still remains an irrefutable fact that the main business of the Valley is the growing of wine grapes and the making of table wines. Trying to narrate the story of the Napa Valley without telling about these things would be like trying to describe Detroit without once mentioning the automobile industry.

Another fact should be made crystal clear. I make no pretense of being a wine expert, a fact which daily becomes more clear to me as I associate with people who are. While I have an excellent cellar, and under the tutelage of some very expert tasters have developed a rather discriminative palate, I do not feel myself qualified to pass judgment on the relative merits of the various wines I have tasted in this valley. Suffice it to say that my interest in wine, and the places where it is produced, has taken me to most of the places on this earth where good wines are made, and not the least of these is the Napa Valley. Certainly, no place has consistently offered me better wine.

In case you're thinking of loading all your worldly possessions onto a truck and heading for the Napa Valley, it's only fair to tell you that those beautiful hills also grow a luxuriant crop of poison oak, the rattlesnakes are downright unsocial, and the drinking water, to put it kindly, is somewhat less than ideal. Traffic on Highway 29 is a weekend nightmare, real estate prices are astronomical and still rising, living costs are soaring,

Flowering mustard frames Alexa Chappellet near her hilltop home at Pritchard Hill. *Right:* The Old Bale Mill was built in 1846 and for many years ground grist and flour. It is now a major tourist attraction and its 40 foot overshot wheel is one of the most popular targets for cameras in all of California.

holding ponds sometimes exude a highly fetid odor, and one must drive sixty miles or so to reach the conveniences of a large metropolitan area.

Somehow, this doesn't seem to deter the flood of people seeking to settle here. Napa Valley was threatened with the fate of San Jose, where one of the most beautifully fertile agricultural areas in California was inexorably swallowed up by urbanization. So, in 1968, an agricultural preserve was established for Napa County, very strictly delineating the conditions under which homes and industries could be built in the Valley. The result has been that from the city of Napa northward, the Valley is still mostly agricultural, and wineries seeking to expand almost drown in a sea of paperwork before they can increase their output. Vineyards seem to have less trouble getting permission, so that occasionally the industry suffers from a surplus of grapes, especially of choice varietals from newly planted vineyards that are just now coming into production. This surplus of grapes presents a problem; in this case too much of a good thing. Wineries will have to be expanded, to house the additional stores of wine, and consumption should be increased, which is not always feasible in the face of rising prices, before this problem is solved. Of course, there will never be a real surplus of the best wines: the total production of the whole Valley is too limited to ever have that happen, and Napa Valley wines are always in demand; but local conditions can create temporary problems, the solution of which can add a few wrinkles to the harried vintner's brow.

Every few miles, along Highway 29, towns are strung like beads on a necklace. These towns are small, and staying small by choice. Yountville is growing eastward, but seems to be well stabilized. Oakville and Rutherford are the very small sites of sizable wineries, while St. Helena and Calistoga seem quite content to remain what they are: rural, quiet towns with vintage 1915 streetlights and well used parks; pages out of a more sedate chapter in American life. These small towns glory in their smallness, and have absolutely no intention of ever achieving the growth that has transformed so much of California into a characterless suburbia.

Unlike the great wine producing areas of Europe, the Napa Valley has a comparatively short wine producing history. The Franciscan missionaries led the way when in 1823 Father Jose Altimira and an armed escort of Mexican soldiers visited the Valley, looking for a site that would complete the chain of missions started by Father Juniperro Serra. Father Altimira finally chose his mission site at Sonoma, where the church he established is today the well visited Mission San Fransisco Solano. He did, however, record his visit to the Napa Valley in such glowing terms that it shortly became the mecca of settlers seeking new wildernesses to conquer.

There is no doubt that it was a wilderness. Part of it was a swamp, teeming with waterfowl and crisscrossed by myriad creeks and sloughs. Much of the valley was covered with veritable jungles of oak trees, and alive with game. Archaeological excavations have shown that this valley has had a continuous occupancy by people for over four thousand years, and it is safe to conjecture that nature's bounty had much to do with their presence. The Indians not only lived very well from this provident land, but also found in the hot springs and mud baths that bubble so profusely from the base of

The White Riesling grape, which is the basis of the great Johannisberger Riesling of Germany, produces, in the Napa Valley, a fruity semi-sweet wine that is probably the most popular of all the white wines produced in this country. *Right:* A volcanic upheaval probably caused this rocky knoll in the Valley. In spite of the difficulties attendant to building on such a site, these are favored building spots, probably because of the beautiful views they afford.

Mt. St. Helena a cure for the multiple aches and pains that always seem to plague a primitive culture. They were generally a peaceful, unwarlike people; clean, moral and with a high regard for the beautiful realm that was their home. Unfortunately, these qualities are no match for the steel and greed of a technologically superior culture, so they were an easy prey to the white men who soon flocked in to work the land grants Mexico was so eager to bestow on loyal citizens who would develop this new land.

The white man brought not only a new way of life; he also brought his diseases against which the Indian had no natural immunity. Smallpox was the most virulent killer, although cholera and venereal diseases also decimated this once happy people. In a century since the coming of the white man, the original several thousands of natives have dwindled down to a comparative handful. Stone artifacts and beautifully chipped arrowheads from the obsidian of Glass Mountain are about the only sign that they have ever lived here, although the present name of the valley itself is of Indian origin.

The Napa Valley fell within the administrative jurisdiction of General Mariano Vallejo, the urbane Mexican military governor whose headquarters were at nearby Sonoma. He was under instructions from his superiors to maintain order, collect taxes, and develop the land. To this end, a loyal citizen of Mexico with the right connections, who indicated that he could, and would, carve a productive, tax-paying ranch out of the wilderness found the acquisition of land not too difficult. The big problem was finding the labor necessary to work such an establishment. The Indians were docile enough, and when correctly supervised made reasonably good agricultural workers. They were, however, inclined to have a rather relaxed attitude toward hard physical labor, expecially when the hunting and the fishing were so good. These pragmatists could see no valid reason to sweat in the fields when Nature's bounty was all around them, free for the taking. It took a special type of man to handle them and that man soon put in an appearance just at the time when the tides of agriculture, already well established in neighboring Sonoma, were lapping closer and closer to the Napa Valley.

This region has produced more than its share of memorable characters, but with the possible exception of the legendary Sam Brannan, none more colorful than George Calvert Yount.

A native of North Carolina, Yount was part of that restless horde that pushed westward in the early part of the nineteenth century always looking for a new frontier. He was a man of his time: energetic, innovative, resourceful, fifty years a pioneer, but when in 1831 he first saw the whole Napa Valley, reportedly after climbing an Indian trail to the top of Mt. St. Helena, he saw a spectacle that must have moved him to the very depths of his soul. The valley was wearing its spring vestments: a bright splash of color from the flowering mustard weed that painted it in a streak of yellow-gold. Instinctively, he knew that his search for a place where he could put down roots was over, that in this beautiful valley he would live and die. He got his wish. The remains of George Yount today rest in Yountville, a valley town named in his honor.

In General Vallejo, the cultured governor of this region, he found a kindred spirit, and this oddly as-

The work is hot, and that lug of grapes weighs forty pounds, but there's always time for a smile. *Right:* Day is dying over the western mountains and the Valley basks in a golden haze. Twilight and dawn are the magic times in a valley that is always beautiful.

sorted pair soon became fast friends. Yount had little in the way of material possessions, but he had the resourcefulness of the pioneer and the uncanny trading ability of the frontiersman. One story of how he built his fortune relates that he once showed the general how the redwood trees that grew in the sheltered mountain valleys of his domains could be readily transformed into shingles that were lighter and generally superior to the baked tile then used in roofing. The general's gratitude took the form of a grant stretching for miles, the Rancho Caymus which now constitutes a good part of the Napa Valley. Yount lived the usual good life of the Spanish land grant rancher, raising cattle, sheep . . ., and grapes, which the general converted to wine in his Mission style winery.

The practice of viticulture was not new in California. The very earliest Franciscan missionaries brought with them cuttings of the Mission grape, which had thrived so mightily in Mexico that the reigning Spanish overlords once had them uprooted because their production threatened the livelihood of Spanish vintners. The highly productive Mission grape, which never yielded a great beverage, was imported to make wine for the Mass. Since crushing was achieved by having Indians dance barefooted on a mass of grapes piled onto a stretched cowhide, and fermentation took place in skin bags with the hair turned inward, there may have been a few reasons other than the quality of the grapes that the wine never achieved a high degree of popularity. But it was wine, and in lieu of something better, it had to do.

As in the days of ancient Rome, the vineyard workers were the natives. Their work produced not only wine, after a fashion, but also a side benefit in that it helped stabilize a sometimes nomadic population, drew off their excess energy in agriculture rather than warfare, and by binding them to the soil, helped accelerate the process of "civilization." Shades of the Roman emperors! The very same reasons had been applied, eighteen centuries before, to settle and civilize the then warlike tribes of Gaul, and in the process produced the people who were to become the world's finest vintners.

Probably because he was himself a frontiersman and had a thorough knowledge of Indian mentality, Yount got along very well with them, and in a short time was able to make them skilled vineyard workers. His vineyards flourished, especially since it soon became very apparent that due to some happy natural circumstance, his grant of land constituted an area supremely well adapted to the raising of superior grapes.

The qualities that were to make the Napa Valley world famous had been discovered.

The next twenty years or so were pretty hectic, for the rush of Forty-niners to the gold fields of the Mother Lodge Country spilled over into the Valley, and almost overnight changed the character of the region. These people had a tendency to blandly ignore property lines, and since they were apt to be a bit careless as well as extremely adept with firearms, the process of removing them from the land was sometimes highly interesting. Then, too, the transition from Mexican to American sovereignty resulted in legal difficulties, disputed land grants, and general uncivility. But somehow by 1860, the problems had been resolved and the Valley was ready to assume its rightful role.

Grapes in a basket, and a freshly opened bottle of Chardonnay are a natural adjunct to a party in the Napa Valley, as are these at Bob Wood's party to celebrate the first crush of the 1974 season. *Right:* A young man practices a very ancient art at the Robert Mondavi Winery. A young cooper assembles barrel staves of Navarre oak imported from France. The tools he is using have changed little in 4,000 years. *Pages 40-41:* From the top of Pritchard Hill the eye roams over acres of beautifully tilled vineyards to Mt. St. Helena, towering in the distance. This scene is beautiful at any time of day, but is particularly entrancing at sunset.

The 1860's saw an influx of European winemakers, usually cultured, knowledgeable men who indelibly stamped the future character of the Valley. The word of this new wine producing region must have reached Germany first, because the initial wave of vintners were mostly Germans. Charles Krug came in 1858, and in 1861 established a solidly built stone winery, part of which still stands to this day. In 1862 Jacob Schram cleared mountain land and planted the vines that were to firmly establish Schramsberg as one of the outstanding wineries of California. The Beringer brothers, Jacob and Frederic were comparatively late comers but they brought with them the kind of winemaking they had learned in the Medoc and profoundly affected the style of viticulture in the Valley. Frederic also brought a style of living whose effect can be felt to this day. On the outskirts of St. Helena, fronting the extensive caves of his winery, he erected a replica of the ancestral home in Mainz, Germany. Resplendent with carved oak and cut glass, it has been beautifully restored to the glory that once made it the social center of St. Helena.

By 1880 winemaking was firmly established as the major occupation of the Valley. No less than six hundred vineyards flourished, and from Napa to Calistoga the valley was clothed in a mantle of vigorously growing vines. In spite of the economic upheavals of the 1870's, the future seemed golden indeed. Napa Valley wines were already establishing their reputation for excellence, the market, though erratic, was good and getting better, and although the industry always had its share of problems, no one could foresee anything but an increasingly prosperous future.

Then, disaster struck.

Imagine the consternation of a vineyardist who has worked ten years or more to establish his vigorously healthy vines and then see them suddenly dry up and die. On pulling up a dying vine, he finds that the root system has been systematically riddled. It has been destroyed, underground, by a pest so small that it can hardly be seen by the naked eye, but the staggering damage that *phylloxera vastatrix* causes is all too apparent! The vine louse probably reached California on the cuttings imported from Europe by Count Agoston Haraszthy but was paradoxically of American origin. The only known method of combating this underground menace was flooding the vineyards long enough to drown the pest but not long enough to rot the vines. While this method may have been sometimes feasible in Europe, it was essentially impractical in Napa Valley, a region noted neither for an excess of water or flat land; and so many a fine vineyard was uprooted and planted to grass.

The cure was found just in time to keep the infant industry from foundering. It was discovered that while phylloxera loves the roots of the vinifera grapes, it could not damage the roots of the native American vines. Centuries of adaptation probably is the reason for this most fortuitous circumstance. The noble grapes of the Old World could be, and were, successfully grafted to the native American rootstock, and within ten years the vineyards were flourishing again. The vineyardists breathed a sigh of relief. Certainly, they thought, nothing could be worse than phylloxera and the financial panics that plagued the era.

They were wrong.

Charles Carpy's grandfather helped to establish the wine industry in the Napa Valley and his grandson carries on the family tradition as one of the partners in Freemark Abbey. *Right:* It's not easy to smile for the photographer when you've been working 10 hours picking grapes, your sunburn is killing you, and that forty pound lug of grapes weighs at least a ton, but Kathie Bissonette can still manage a smile as she totes a lug of Chardonnay grapes from the slopes of Chateau Chevalier's vineyards. *Pages 44-45:* Vineyards run abruptly into the eastern mountain wall, a short distance off the Silverado Trail, on a side road leading to Stag's Leap Winery.

On October 18, 1919, to the utter disbelief of this wine producing area, the 18th Amendment, which prohibited the manufacture, sale, or transportation of intoxicating liquor was ratified and became national law, even in the Napa Valley. To a people for whom wine was a staple, and a way of life, this was complete madness: a well intentioned, but senseless, completely unworkable regulation whose only function seemed to be the ruination of the work of generations and to make a lawbreaker out of anyone who did the major part of that work.

Any law, to be functional, must have the support of the general populace, and in no section of the United States was the Prohibition Amendment more enthusiastically ignored than in the Napa Valley. It seemed no Italian ever could be convinced that this was really the law of the land and that in ignoring it he was committing a serious crime. However, after a few painful incidents, it finally dawned on them that this was not some monstrous practical joke, that they were indeed breaking the law by practicing the art that had been handed down to them by their ancestors for two thousand years. Sadly, they began to convert their beautifully tended vineyards to prune and walnut orchards.

To be sure, some wineries, especially those that had wisely specialized in sacramental and medicinal wines kept going all through Prohibition, and so kept alive the art of the vintner. Then, too, the hills around St. Helena and Calistoga are rugged and not too easily accessible to those not familiar with them. Old timers will tell you stories of tank car loads of molasses moving into the valley . . . every two or three days, to be fermented and distilled into 190 proof alcohol that could be cut back to potable strength. Stills were everywhere, and the heady odor of fermenting wine that had formerly clothed the valley was replaced by the equally heady odor of fermenting mash and distilled moonshine. Very heavy coffins, followed by sad faced mourners, routinely went to Santa Rosa to be placed on the train to San Francisco. Of course, those coffins sloshed a bit when jostled and the same mourners attended each funeral, a fact that was dutifully pointed out by a local man who was doing his last two years in Federal service before claiming his pension. Following his cue the mourners were changed, and he lived to claim his pension.

Those barely accessible mountain vineyards really came into their own during Prohibition. Many a fine vintage was gathered, crushed and fermented in the dark of the moon so that when the national madness passed in 1933, there were some well aged wines on hand to toast its unlamented demise.

There is no denying that Prohibition did more damage to the Napa Valley than even the phylloxera beetle. Beautifully tended vineyards of prime varietal grapes were ripped up to be replanted with prunes, walnuts, or sowed to pasture grass. Vacated wineries fell into disrepair or were converted to other uses. Irreplaceable old cooperage fell apart, and was lost forever. A vineyard that produces no grapes, or a winery that makes no wine is an exercise in futility. These were undeniably disasters, but the bigger loss was in people. An unemployed vinter must necessarily find other work if he is to survive, and skills unused for fourteen years can become so atrophied that their revival is questionable. Also, good vineyard workers are not produced overnight.

Erected in 1890, this charming old stone building in Calistoga now houses a goldsmith's shop. *Right:* An old remodeled winery has been turned into a charming warren of shops, boutiques and restaurant at Yountville's Vintage 1870 complex.

A whole generation of skilled workers in fine varietal grapes was lost, and those who survived by tending the Alicante Bouschet grape lost a virtue very important to a skilled craftsman: his pride in his work. This tough skinned but quite plebeian grape largely supplanted the more delicate varietal grapes because it could stand the rigors of transportation even to the East Coast. There it was used for home winemaking, which was legal under this peculiar law. The Alicante was also a great favorite with bootleggers because its blood-red juice imparted a lot of color to the wine, and so could be liberally "cut" with adulterants and still present a passable color to the undiscerning eye. Large quantities of this very inferior wine were consumed, and tended to set standards that were so low that when the horrible post-Prohibition wines arrived, they were accepted, if not with enthusiasm, at least with resignation.

Another, if somewhat intangible loss was the general disregard for law engendered by Prohibition. People who had never before broken a major law now did so with little or no compunction, and the habit inevitably spread to all fields of endeavor, business and social. Gangsters accumulated huge fortunes and invested them in extralegal enterprises, operating behind the shield of bought public officials and judges. The general decline in morality that began during Prohibition seeded a bitter harvest, the effects of which are still with us today and influence our everyday lives. Those fourteen years of Prohibition can truly be called the Napa Valley's—and America's—Dark Age.

The aftermath of Prohibition was almost as ruinous to the industry as the law itself had been. The great thirst engendered by the long dry spell had to be quenched somehow, and wines whose only distinction was that they had a very high alcoholic content were rushed into production. People who had never tasted wine before may very well be excused if, when tasting some of those first efforts, they concluded that they had not been missing very much. Cheaply made, poorly aged wines undeniably sold, but also created a negative reaction that set back for many years the general acceptance of wine as a worthwhile experience.

However, along with the poor wines, some good and even great wines were being laid down. Now that wine production could function legally, new wineries were opened, modern methods were introduced, and the foundations for the present high standards now prevalent in the Valley were formulated. Wineries proliferated, and every year more and more acreage in the Valley was dedicated to grape growing. The process of 1919 was now being reversed: extensive, well established groves of prunes and walnuts were being torn out and the ground painstakingly prepared for the vines that would supply the grapes the wineries needed to supply an ever expanding market.

The modern era of the Napa Valley had begun.

A few far sighted vintners as far back as 1943 had already perceived the obvious. The future of the Valley should rest on the solid base of quality rather than quantity. After all, even if all the arable land in the Valley were to be planted to grapes, there would be a total of only about 25,000 acres: an area that could comfortably be tucked into a forgotten corner of Bordeaux. By this time, all sections of the Valley had been planted to grapes of one variety or another, and a pat-

One of the most overlooked floral displays in botanical history is the flowering of the grape, here shown larger than life size. However, without this insignificant looking display, there would be no ripe grapes in September. *Right:* Under an arch of olive trees, planted a hundred years ago by Jacob Schram, the Jack Davies family, present owners of Schramsberg, head happily back home after a day's outing in the vineyards.

tern was beginning to emerge. The three hundred or so micro-climates into which the Valley is divided were beginning to be discovered and to assert themselves. Some sections raised exceptional Zinfandel, others through some unique chemistry did better with White Riesling, while in a third Cabernet Sauvignon thrived best. The southern end of the Valley, around Carneros, cooled as it is by the fogs of San Pablo Bay, produced a very superior Pinot Noir, while up in the mountains the Christian Brothers lovingly cared for their Pinot St. George and Fred McCrea was raising the Chardonnay that was establishing a national reputation for his Stony Hill winery.

And so it goes today, but always the quantities are fairly small, because we are dealing here with noble grapes that have a relatively light yield, even in the fertile soil of the Napa Valley. It is a natural setting for an emphasis on quality rather than quantity, and in the short time that this concept has been established it has already emphatically proved that it was the right step to take.

Not so long ago, Sutter Home Winery, a small family operation in St. Helena, used to boast that if you could roll your container through the front door, they'd fill it with a very fine Zinfandel for seventy five cents a gallon. They still make very fine Zinfandel, but now it is carefully bottled and labelled with their own name, and the former price is now just a lovely memory. The conversion of a people traditionally conservative and bound more to the production of a fine wine than to the marketing thereof didn't come easily, or overnight. For many years fine wine had been made and sold by the jug, or barrel, anonymously, to some wholesaler who put his own label on it, and trusted to his promotional skill to make the label known . . . always hoping that he could get a further supply of that wine next year to supply the customers who had become accustomed to it.

But now, a new concept was being born. As far back as 1889, Gustave Niebaum of Inglenook had proved that wine produced in the Napa Valley could not only hold its own in competition with the world's finest, but would come home with a favorably disproportionate share of the gold medals. Here in this valley was a unique combination of soil, climate, grapes and people that resulted in wine equal or superior to that produced anywhere else. It took courage to break the iron mold set down by generations of vintners raised in the tradition that the world's greatest wines were products of France, Germany or Italy; but here was positive proof that in this small valley in the New World, wine of top premium quality could, and was, being consistently made.

A proud heritage was taking shape. Today, the words "Napa Valley" on a wine label are the cachet of assured quality, and the whole industry owes a debt to those workers who have labored so indefatigably not only to produce a superior vintage product, but also to promote it as such.

The last ten years or so have witnessed dramatic changes in the ownership patterns of the Valley's wineries. In 1964 Inglenook, one of the fine old family owned wineries was sold to United Vintners, and in 1969 Beaulieu Vineyards was bought by Heublein Inc., Pillsbury acquired a majority interest in Souverain, and Beringer became part of the huge Nestle conglomerate.

Inglenook's tiled roof is a Valley landmark, especially from the back side of the winery. This is one roof the flickers can't attack, although they've been known to try. *Right:* Near the Yountville crossroad, the vineyards are bounded by ancient stone walls built by Chinese labor, and huge old eucalyptus trees whose predecessors were imported from Australia for timber.

The change from family ownership to control by large corporations has had, and inevitably will have, a decided effect on the future of the Valley, with positive and negative aspects rather effectively balancing each other. The greatest fear held by many Valley inhabitants is that decisions vitally affecting the Valley will no longer be entirely made here, but by officers in some far away board room who will not be as sensitive to local conditions as they would be if they lived here. The firms that are under conglomerate control are large, respected businesses with good customer acceptance and established reputations. Any cheapening of these firms' products to trade on a past reputation would be a serious blow to the Napa Valley's reputation for excellence, and there is always a fear that a desire for a profitable balance sheet may induce such a move, especially in a softening market.

The other side of the coin is that the large corporations are well aware of the value of the Napa Valley appellation: this was a large part of the reason for acquisition, and they are too smart to kill the goose that lays golden eggs. In at least one instance, a large corporation took an established label whose wine had begun a drop in quality and by the infusion of large quantities of corporate money had brought in the talent, equipment, and vineyards it took to not only stop the slide, but to bring that label back to its former peak. Now, their effort is to surpass that peak, and if it takes money to do that, it is available, and in any necessary amount.

Plant modernization takes money: large sums of money. The corporations have been generous with their expansions and improvements, and in the process are adding luster to the Napa Valley name. Then, too, marketing systems and much improved distribution spread the word that "Napa Valley" means quality. These are accomplishments beyond the reach of the smaller winery, which must rely mainly on word of mouth for its advertising. The large corporations, by effective utilization of their much larger resources can give the whole Valley a boost that will materially help everyone in it, big and small alike.

Another, not so well known facet of the corporate presence is the stabilizing effect they have on prices. In 1974, the valley produced a very large crop of wine grapes, partly because of a good growing season, but also because much new acreage has reached the bearing stage. These added grapes could very well have stayed on the vine, unpicked, if larger corporations such as Allied Vintners, Napa Valley Co-op, and the Christian Brothers with their huge processing facilities had not stepped into the breach and siphoned off the grapes that would have completely glutted the market. Then, too, most corporations faced as they were by a sometimes hostile attitude at the times of their acquisitions were forced to plant their own vineyards to insure their supply. Those vineyards are bearing now, and by relieving a bit of the pressure on the smaller wineries, help them to get a price they can live with for the grapes they need.

Probably the most propitious sign that the corporations want to get along with their neighbors in the Valley and be accepted as part of the community is the active interest they are taking in local activities and problems. Managers are usually alert to the good public relations that can accrue from such activity, and are

Bob Trinchero adjusts the must pipe that feeds pulped grapes into the fermentation tank. The whole family works in this firm, one of the truly family operated wineries in the Valley. *Right:* The morning mists hang low over the valley until dissipated by the midmorning sun. This touch of coolness adds complexity to the wine, in the form of fruit acid.

very generous with their time and facilities. The corporations are well represented in the Napa Valley Vintners' association and mingle on an equal footing with the very smallest wineries represented by that group. In turn, the fears and worries that were attendant to the coming of the corporations are at least partly allayed. After all, there is a very good precedent. The Christian Brothers, a tax-paying corporation of some considerable size, has been a part of the Valley scene since 1930, and no group is more respected or held in higher esteem.

There is a nucleus of family owned wineries in the Valley that has so far resisted all offers tendered to them that would make them instant millionaires and effectively deprive them of their major reason for living. With these people, the making of fine wine is more an obsession than it is a job: they probably would be winemakers even if they were not being paid for it, simply because they love their life, and the place where they live it. It is also probably no coincidence that these people work sixteen hours a day, thrive on it, and every year are making a good product better.

The exhilarating part of opening up new frontiers of quality is that each time some obstacle is surmounted, a whole new vista is opened: there are new heights to be scaled, and old standards to be exceeded. With each victory comes the attendant euphoric feeling of accomplishment, so that the wines that were good enough yesterday are not nearly good enough today. For that reason the track is getting faster every year, and a host of eager young vintners are snapping at the leaders who must run faster than ever just to stay in place. The net result, of course, is better wine, and a greater utilization of the unique qualities that make this valley such an exciting place in which to live.

The future promises to be anything but dull: the Valley is in very good hands.

Zinfandel is a favorite grape with the pickers. The clusters are fairly large and usually easily accessible. *Right:* An ancient stonewall's stark lines are softened by the beauty of California poppies on the Oakville Crossroad. *Pages 56-57:* Safely into the crusher at last; red wine grapes reach the last stage in the complicated cycle where they trade one life as grapes for another as wine.

After all the juice has been extracted from the must there is still use for the residue. Called "pomace" it makes an excellent, as well as colorful, vineyard fertilizer. *Left:* From a rocky knoll near his home and doing what comes naturally at his age, Tom Gamble gets a boy's eye view of the Napa Valley. *Pages 60-61:* It looks like something transplanted complete from some Aegean isle, but Sterling Vineyards Winery is really an ultra-modern complex, dedicated to the making of good wine. It was also designed to give the tourist a good idea of how that wine is made.

CHAPTER I

LAND OF THE SMOKING EARTH, CALISTOGA

When you consider that Calistoga was founded by the empire-building Sam Brannan you have a right to expect something out of the ordinary. Sam was the stuff of which legends are spun, and the town he founded just naturally is as distinctive and unique as he was. A beautifully situated small town of 1800 delightfully chauvinistic souls, it sits at the head of the Napa Valley with Mt. St. Helena towering in its back yard. Deservedly proud of its legendary past, it is perfectly content with its very agreeable present, and serenely confident in its promising future.

Sam Brannan certainly thought it had a good future, and that is why with the whole West to choose from, he chose this spot to crown the career that had made him, at 28, California's first millionaire, and as intriguing a figure as this picturesque valley has ever produced. A renegade Mormon who found horse racing, wine drinking, and wooing the prettiest women in the West more to his liking than hard manual work, he was also a charismatic leader, a far sighted entrepreneur, the possessor of a raffish if somewhat ebullient charm, and a very hard worker whenever the labor happened to be to his liking. Sam was first and foremost a promoter; one of that breed of men who carved an empire out of a wilderness and indelibly stamped a region with the brand of his personality. In the Calistoga region, he saw a chance to crown his career with an enterprise in keeping with the flamboyance that had carried him to fame and fortune.

The Indians had for centuries used the mud baths and goethermal springs that bubble from the base of Mt. St. Helena as a remedy for arthritic pain. It was therefore a popular gathering spot, in theory a place where tribal animosities were suspended, or at least curtailed, but in actual fact the scene of many a pitched battle. Because of the many thermal springs in this area, some of them gushing plumes of live steam, the Indians referred to this are as "The Land Of The Smoking Earth."

The potential for recreation and development was tremendous, but it took a man of Brannan's vision and enthusiasm to transform the potential into reality. The fact that he had six million dollars to pour into the venture certainly didn't hurt any; and he needed a good part of that money, for when Sam dreamed, he dreamed on a big scale; and what he envisioned was a spa to rival any then in existence. Starting in 1860, he poured money into a complex of swimming pools, cottages, mud baths and roller skating rinks. Avenues planted with palm trees led to the various parts of the estate, and to the race track where his blooded Arabian horses regularly ran in the wildest races the Valley has ever seen. The whole place was designed to attract the newly rich aristocracy of San Francisco, and no money was spared to build a place where they would feel at home.

The aristocracy of San Francisco stayed away in droves. Sam's reputation as a lady's man, carouser, and general hell-raiser was not exactly the mark of distinction that the newly respectable elite of the Bay City craved. True, many of them spent a surreptitious week or two at Brannan's, and went home wonderfully refreshed, but the place never did receive the cachet of

Hanns Kornell could easily delegate this task to someone else, but he personally examines each bottle of champagne by the traditional method: viewing the refracted light of candle flame through the wine to be sure it meets his exacting standards for clarity and lack of deposit. *Right:* At Hanns Kornell's Larkmead Lane champagne cellars, over a million bottles of fine sparkling wine rest and bottle age. Periodically, Hanns inspects, tests and tastes, to make sure that his "children are growing up properly".

respectability Sam so earnestly sought . . . at least, not during his life time . . . After he left the operation it became quite the gathering place for people not only from the Bay area, but from the whole country.

There are several stories of how the town got its name. Before Brannan's time, the settlement had been named "Agua Caliente," an obvious reference to the many hot water springs in the area. The most usual story tells how the round of celebrations marking the opening of the new resort obviously entailed the consumption of other, stronger waters, for during the course of a decidedly bibulous dedication Brannan proposed a toast to the new enterprise "The Saratoga of California." His usually nimble tongue somewhat paralyzed by the local wine, it came out as "Calistoga of Sarafornia."

The intriguing name stuck.

For forty years, Calistoga was a popular resort, if not with the elite of California, at least with enough people to spread its fame liberally. People took the train from a landing on San Pablo Bay and travelled the length of the lovely Napa Valley to Calistoga. On returning, they brought back with them one of the habits contracted at Brannan's resort: a taste for the local wine. Sam Brannan had early realized the Valley's potential for producing fine wine, and by the mid 1860's his vineyards were the Valley's finest, boasting of 125,000 vines. With his usual business acumen, he certainly saw to it that his wines were served in the right places, and while the San Francisco aristocracy may have looked askance at Sam and his escapades, they readily accepted the quality of what he bottled. Napa Valley wines had an early acceptance in San Francisco, in spite of the snobbery of the times that insisted nothing was as good as the best Bordeaux or Burgundy.

Although Calistoga has long ago ceded the title of "Wine Center of the Valley" to nearby St. Helena, it still maintains a lively interest in things vinous. On Tubbs Lane, at the northern edge of the town, Chateau Montelena, an imposing French style chateau built by European stonemasons with imported stone, produces outstanding varietal wines. Beautifully situated on the edge of an artificial lake that boasts authentic Chinese pagodas, it is a delightful spot for a picnic, and one that has yet to be fully discovered. The winemaker is Mike Grgich, an extrovert Croatian with a positive genius for producing fine wines, which his sales manager Mike Golick markets with style and a distinctive flair. A delightful place to visit any time of the year, but especially on a warm summer day, where it is a cool oasis in an otherwise decidedly hot area.

At the southern end of Calistoga, and some few miles down the valley, Sterling Vineyards crowns its wooded knoll, looking like a picture out of an Aegean Sea travelogue. Certainly the most spectacular setting in the valley, it was engineered to be not only a highly functional winery, but also a showplace where visitors could, on an unescorted tour, see all phases of winemaking and storage. A monocable tramway feeds visitors to the attractively situated tasting room, and also serves the function of keeping the too casual visitor at the bottom of the mountain. The view from the terraces of Sterling is the best in the whole valley, and worth in itself the cost of the trip. Sterling produces excellent varietal wines that are available at the winery and in

At the Charles Krug Winery a gondola load of red grapes is tipped into the crusher by a movable hoist. The screw at the bottom of the crusher will feed the grapes into the crushing mechanism where the fruit is pulped. *Right:* The barrel-aging room at Sterling Vineyards is a study in symmetry, enhanced with light colored by stained glass windows. In this small cooperage, wines sleep, sometimes for years, until they gain the smoothness and character that oak supplies so graciously.

selected California restaurants, although some wines will be marketed through distributors as this new winery achieves its full potential.

On the eastern edge of the Valley, near the Silverado trail, the spanking new Cuvaison Winery, an outstanding piece of functional Mission-style architecture nestles into the hillside, looking as though it had grown there, so beautifully have its lines been integrated with the surrounding terrain.

Most of the Calistoga area wineries take advantage of the fact that red wine grapes attain a high sugar content at this end of the Valley, probably because climatically the north end of the Valley is much warmer. The south end is cooled, morning and evening, by the fogs off San Pablo Bay and so does not ripen grapes as quickly as does the more sunshiny north end. Also, the rocks rimming Calistoga retain the afternoon heat, and by radiating it long into the evening hasten the ripening process by providing a high and long caloric intake. Some grapes, Zinfandel for instance, seem to do better on slopes, and there are slopes all around Calistoga.

Some of those slopes become rather precipitous. Mt. St. Helena itself is a semi-extinct volcano with some very abrupt escarpments, and the mountains ringing the valley to the east are sheer rock cliffs many hundreds of feet high. This accounts for the fact that Calistoga is a Sailplaning center. On any warm day these graceful long-winged gliders can be seen effortlessly wheeling and soaring in a breathtakingly beautiful ballet as they seek the rising thermals that will give them altitude.

Not all the wines produced in this area are red. The road leading from Calistoga to St. Helena offers such an intriguing and ever changing panorama that you could be forgiven if you miss the side road to the right with a simple sign beside it that says in elegant cursive script "Schramsberg." That would be your loss, for although the Valley is an undeniably beautiful jewel, there are also facets in the foothills that are equally brilliant, and Schramberg is one of these.

The original vineyard was hacked out of a mixed redwood, oak, and madrona forest by Jacob Schram, who in 1862, started a winery that soon established its reputation as one of the finest in California. When a casual visitor named Robert Louis Stevenson visited the place in 1880, he found the site a picture of prosperity, with a large Victorian mansion and extensive aging cellars carved hundreds of feet into the hillside. Phylloxera and Prohibition dealt the lovely old estate severe blows, but in 1964 Jack and Jamie Davies bought it, and energetically set about restoring it. The place was a ruin, with bats in the attic and rats entrenched in the cellar, but today the old Victorian Mansion has been restored to a thing of beauty. The tunnels have been refurbished, the mountain vineyards replanted, and Jack makes champagne that is pure gold. Using the original French methode champenoise, he produces champagne from Pinot Noir, Pinot Chardonnay, Gamay and Flora grapes that has attracted world wide interest, especially since personnel of the U.S. State Department have been known to order it for the very highest occasions. Jack's training in business management equips him well for the distribution of his scarce champagne is as important as its production. Jacob Schram would be proud to see the estate today—it is in very capable hands.

Louis Martini carries on the tradition established by his late father, one of the greats in the industry. Here, in his laboratory, he checks a wine with a very competent swirl of his glass. *Right:* From the heights of Sterling Vineyards, the Valley spreads its checkerboard of green, gold and crimson.

On the lyrically named Larkmead Lane Hanns Kornell works his magic on a million or so bottles of fine champagne and proudly directs a very solvent empire founded on his skill as a winemaker and his value as a person. A refugee from Hitler's Germany, his is one of the outstanding success stories of the Valley, for from his start in 1940 to the present day, he has built the name "Kornell" into a synonym for fine champagne and staunch integrity. His old stone winery, acquired in 1958 serves as a storehouse and aging cellar for fine wines, mostly Rieslings and Chardonnays which he buys from selected vintners, and using the methode champenoise transforms into sparkling wines that have won many medals, even in competition with the most entrenched champagnes of Europe.

Each part of the Napa Valley is different, has its own attraction, and is an integral part of that enchantment the Napa Valley as a whole weaves so effortlessly. Calistoga, with its Western style buildings, its plumes of geothermal steam, its air of living easily with a very lively past while courting a sedate future, is an intriguing place. What other town of 1800 people can boast of two Russian Orthodox churches, and having been founded by a renegade Mormon who was a con artist beyond compare? A walk through the hillside pioneer cemetery at the edge of town is a walk back into the nineteenth century, yet, lifting your eyes, you see, gliding gracefully in azure skies, sailplanes manned by bronzed young men and women who proudly call this place home, and feel they have the best of all worlds.

It is seemingly paradoxical that Calistoga, at the very edge of the wine country and with a history of viticulture, should also be home to an excellent institution dedicated to the rehabilitation of those who have become too fond of the grape. It is part of the character of this town that seems to take the best from all facets of our culture, blend it with its own particular style of living, and in so doing produce a way of life that is an intrinsic and fascinating part of the Napa Valley.

Through the open porch of Sterling Vineyards Winery, one sees the arches and architecture that have so often made this winery compared to a Greek monastery. *Right:* Large oaken casks at Sterling Vineyards Winery store a wealth of aging wine; and also provide a dramatic setting for the light streaming through the colored windows of the cellar.

The hillside vineyards of Stony Hill are famous in the industry, in that they produce superlative Chardonnay. Production at this tiny winery is so limited that grapes are gathered in lug boxes and transported to the winery on the hood of a 1943 vintage Army Jeep, which is probably the best possible vehicle for this rugged terrain. *Right:* Jets of geo-thermal steam issue from pipes sunk into the ground at Pacheteau's Resort, in Calistoga. This is the area promoted by Sam Brannan, and was a leading spa for many years. *Pages 72-73:* In the cool caves of Schromsberg, bins of bottles patiently sleep and let their contents achieve the nobility which is their rightful due.

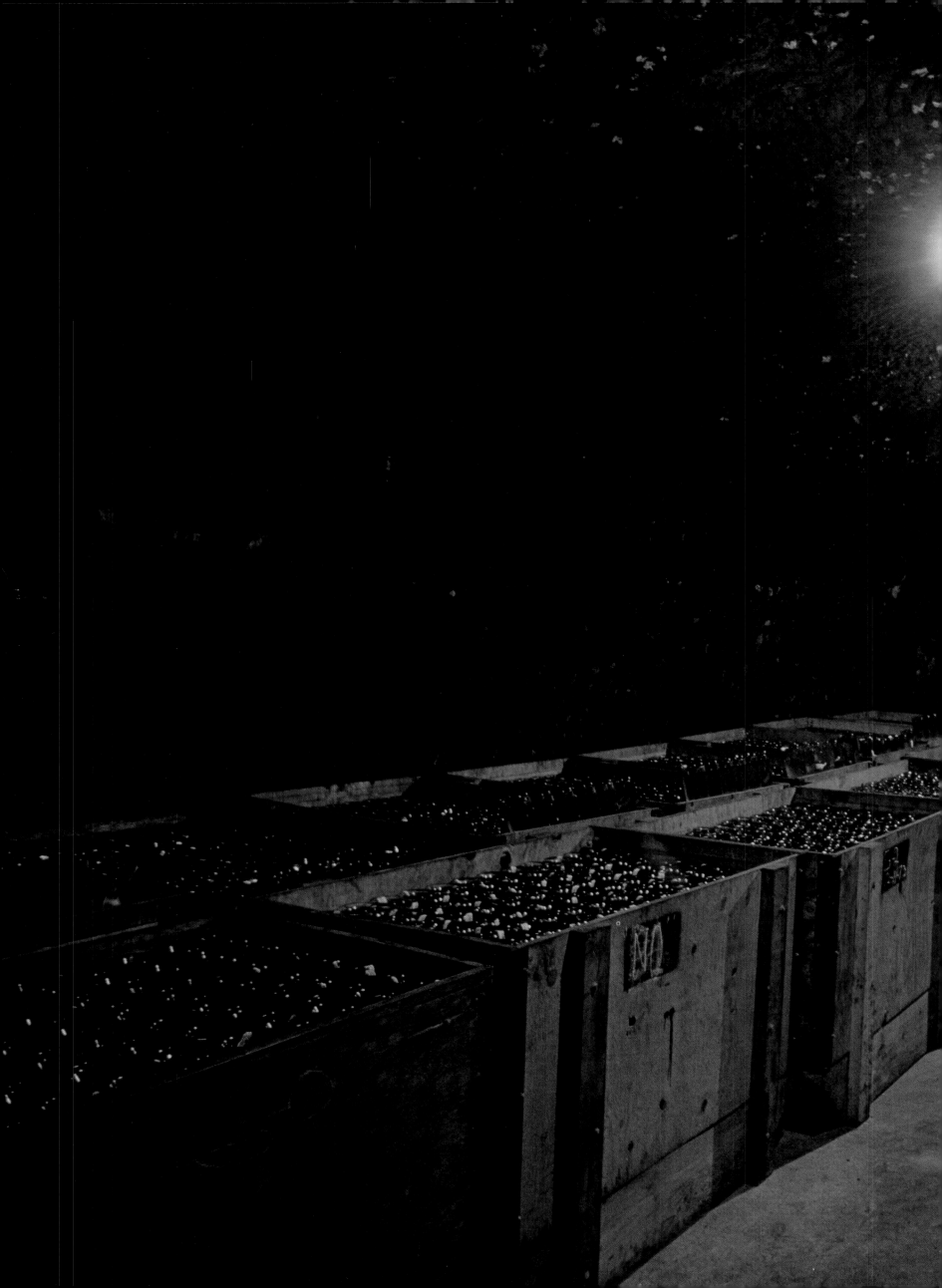

CHAPTER II

HEART OF THE VALLEY — ST. HELENA

It quite commonly happens that people seeing St. Helena for the first time fall helpless victims to its charm. For most, it is an unrequited love, and they return to their own homes with the memory of a pretty, leisurely paced little town that seems to have somehow escaped the frenetic rush of modern times, and has survived as an oasis of peace, quiet, and gracious living. Some determined souls do something about it, for many of the civic leaders of the town are people who have moved into it, and found that while St. Helena indeed lives up to its first impression, it is a quality which is maintained only at the cost of considerable effort.

St. Helena didn't just happen: it is what it is only because of the stamp put on it generations ago by the talented, hardworking men and women who made this their home, the scene of their labors, and established a delightful way of life that persists to this day. It remains as it is only because its present inhabitants appreciate that way of life, and do as little as possible to disturb it.

A fortuitous accident of nature shaped St. Helena's destiny. The soil of the Napa Valley, composed as it is of volcanic dust, sedimentary deposits, and alluvial fans deposited in the valley by the raging mountain streams forms a terrain ideal for the growing of premier quality wine grapes. Add to this the happy chance that the amount of rainfall is usually just right and comes at the proper time, the balance of sunshine and fog is ideal, and numerous micro-climates allow several varieties of fine wine grapes to thrive, and the town's future became predictable. It was foreordained that St. Helena should become the wine capital of California.

It undeniably has. This small town is home base for many a nationally known wine firm whose name is familiar to anyone who has ever shopped for a bottle of fine American wine.

It wasn't always thus. Back in the 1830's when the first white settlers began to enter the valley, their main interest was more in cattle, not primarily for their meat, but for their hides and tallow. The many oak trees in the valley provided the oak bark necessary for the tanning process, and "Napa Leather," most likely first made from deerskins, became a name in the trade that persists to this day. In 1846 Dr. Edward Turner Bale built his grist mill, still standing on the northern edge of St. Helena, which later ground poultry and livestock feed as well as flour for the bread hungry Forty-niners. The old mill, with its giant overshot wheel is today a prime tourist attraction, but in the days of its active life it was a symbol of the things that made life possible and profitable in the Napa Valley.

A short distance south of the old Bale Mill on the opposite side of the road, there sits a handsome building of reddish cut stone. This is Freemark Abbey, which houses not only a nationally famous winery, but also a fine restaurant, a gift shop and a candle factory whose artistic products are world famous. The building dates back to 1895, and an Italian named Antonio Forni, who, like most of the new arrivals from Italy, had wine on his mind. He built well. The old winery, which has passed through many hands before being acquired in 1967 by the present owners has been equipped with the

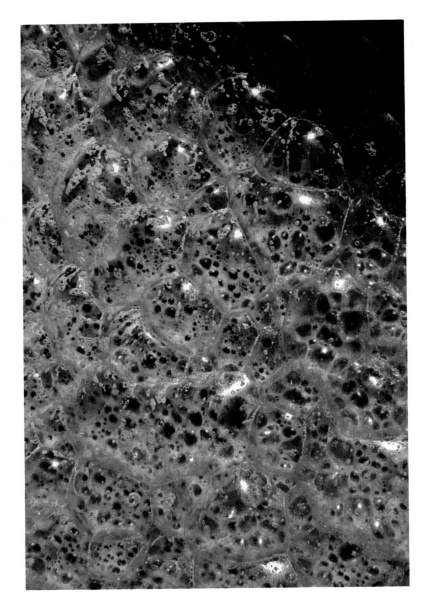

New wine, still frothing from the carbon dioxide attendant to its birth, makes a swirling pink pattern in a wine sump. *Right:* An experimental pressing of Cabernet Franc, at Spring Mountain Winery is part of the experimentation that is always going on at any good winery. Small batches, such as here, are pressed in basket presses rather than in the bladder presses customarily used for the commercial loads. *Pages 76-77:* Jade Lake is a charming little oasis on Tubbs Lane, Calistoga, right next to Chateau Montelena. The islands boast authentically Chinese pagodas and a bottle of chilled white wine is available only a few yards away. Welcome!

latest stainless steel fermentors and is busily fulfilling the reason for which it was originally built: making good wine.

In 1861 Charles Krug built his first permanent winery, north of St. Helena, where part of it stands to this day, the old buildings of greyish stone and stucco blending perfectly with the background of oaks and spacious lawns. The old carriage house that formerly housed the winery's horses now holds hundreds of barrels of aging wine, and the main winery building holds huge tanks, some of redwood and others of glass-lined steel, most of them bigger than a railroad tank car.

The winery was acquired in 1943 by the late Cesare Mondavi; his wife Rosa is still president of the company. Their son, Peter, supervises this, one of the larger wineries in the valley, and keeps an eagle eye on the quality that has made Charles Krug a name that means unvarying excellence.

Across the road from Charles Krug, on a hillside overlooking the Valley, William Bourn, one of the richest men in America in 1889 poured millions into a huge cut stone building that is still the world's largest stone winery. An impressive, cream colored structure crammed with priceless old cooperage it is the aging cellar for the Christian Brothers wineries, and also houses their Charmat process champagne facilities. Daily tours are available through this beautiful old building, which is certainly one of the most impressive in the State, and well worthy of an extended visit.

Only a few hundred yards down the road is the famed Rhine House of the Beringer Brothers Winery. A copy of the ancestral home in Mainz, Germany, it was built of imported German oak and stained glass, and is one of the more impressive sights in the Napa Valley. The famed sandstone caves of the Beringers, patiently hacked out with pick and shovel by Chinese laborers serve as aging cellars for the winery, and have been expertly restored. They are unquestionably one of the more worthwhile tourist attractions of the valley.

Since its acquisition by Nestle's, Beringer has undergone much expansion and renovation. The famed caves have been restored, and banks of new stainless steel fermentors flank each side of the road. Under wine master Myron Nightengale, one of the most respected men in the business, the capacity of the winery has been greatly increased over the old days, but always with the aim of getting the very best quality out of the grapes grown in Beringer's extensive vineyards.

Across the Valley, just off the road to Angwin, Burgess Cellars, a delightfully situated old cut-stone winery perches on its hillside overlooking its own vineyards and enjoys a gorgeous view of the valley, right from its own windows. On the opposite side of the valley, Chateau Chevalier, a delightful replica of a French Chateau sits in fold in a valley off the Spring Mountain road. Greg and Kathie Bissonette have worked long hard hours to replant the mountain vineyards and restore the old estate that had been pretty well reclaimed by the surrounding forest. The grapes are crushed, fermented and aged in the cellar of the picturesque old chateau which not only looks like a French wine cellar, but also functions as one.

The largest home in St. Helena is the huge Victorian mansion erected on Spring Mountain in 1885 by Tiburcio Parrot, the son of the American consul in Mazatlan,

This avenue of elms, fronting the Rhine House in St. Helena, is a cool tunnel of verdure even on the hottest summer day. *Right:* The new buildings of Souverain Winery, on the eastern slopes of the Valley, bask in the warm sun of late afternoon.

and a Mexican mother. A larger replica of the Rhine House, it sits on spacious landscaped grounds overlooking a swimming pool and beautiful view of the Valley. Purchased in 1974 by Mike Robbins, a San Francisco businessman turned winemaker, it will be extensively renovated and house his Spring Mountain Winery, which presently occupies the cellar of another large Victorian house he owns on the St. Helena highway. On the Spring Mountain property is a large tunnel dug ninety feet into the hillside, which affords a perfect spot for aging the Cabernets and Chardonnays that are already establishing an outstanding reputation for this fine winery.

The ride up Spring Mountain road is one of the prettiest originating in the Valley. Densely wooded most of the way, the road is a tunnel of cool verdure, with a lively creek noisily gamboling alongside. Each side road leads to a vineyard or winery, for this whole area is excellent grape growing country, and owners of this choice land are not about to pass up the opportunities that come with the ownership of these coveted spots. The road finally tops the mountain and wanders off downhill to Santa Rosa.

St. Helena is home to two large co-operatives that crush an impressive part of the Valley's total crop. Their large, down to earth exteriors hide really impressive interiors well suited for their purpose, which is to make wine. The relics of an era more dedicated to efficiency rather than aesthetics, they are nevertheless an integral part of the wine complex in the Napa Valley.

On the southern edge of town is a low, very modern complex of buildings that house the warehousing and crushing facilities of the Christian Brothers. This crushing and fermenting complex is quite different in that it is circular, rather than following the more traditional rectangular concept. This innovative step has proven extremely practical, and is always considered as a model whenever new crushing facilities are planned anywhere. Geared to mass production while still keeping all the good aspects of a smaller winery, this modern plant can crush thousands of tons of grapes in the same time most wineries would use to crush a hundred tons. The largest single facility in the Napa Valley, it is nevertheless only part of a planned complex that will some day move the greater part of the Brothers' facilities to South St. Helena.

Their neighbor down the road is the Louis Martini Winery, which is almost always a surprise to the visitor. The name is well known to most wine buffs, who know that for years the name Martini has stood for an always sound, and often great wine at a reasonable price. The buildings were erected in 1933 in anticipation of the end of Prohibition, and are simply no nonsense, practical type structures whose only function is to protect the wine making equipment from the elements. The elder Martini, who established this winery, was a legend in his own time, a hard working, knowledgeable, hospitable Italian who had a positive genius for producing fine wines. His son, Louis P. Martini, who presently heads the operation, has apparently inherited his father's flair and embellished it with a few additional flourishes of his own. A large-framed, energetic man with a ready smile and a notable sense of humor, he is dedicated to carrying on a fine tradition and adding laurels to a name already extremely well respected in wine circles.

In his Spring Mountain vineyard, Jerry Draper squeezes grape-juice onto the plate of his refractometer to measure sugar content. *Right:* Charles Wagner, Jr. is a third generation Valley resident who intends to follow in his father's footsteps and carry on the family's wine-making tradition at Caymus Vineyards. Using a wine-thief, he samples a Pinot Noir that he had a hand in making.

Martini Winery has the usual complement of redwood tanks, only more so. It also has huge concrete vats used for fermenting red wines, and many thousands of oak barrels where red wines, and some whites, patiently sleep and take on the character and silkiness that oak seems to impart so beautifully. Throughout the industry, the name is respected for the integrity and value it implies, for Martini's influence has done much to stabilize prices in this country. A firm believer in giving the customer his money's worth, he is making and selling good wine at a reasonable price . . . and making a profit on it. The influence this has had on stabilizing prices is considerable, for Martini is one of the larger wineries in the Valley, with an output of more than 250,000 cases a year.

Across the street from Martini, Bob Trinchero operates Sutter Home Winery, one of the smaller, more picturesque home type wineries on Highway 29. Starting with a venerable ruin of a building in 1943, the Trinchero family has patiently built it up, year by year, replacing old cooperage with stainless steel fermentors and oaken aging tanks till they today have a functional winery that is an intriguing blend of the latest equipment cheek by jowl with some that would qualify for space in a museum . . . but which nevertheless fulfills its function. This winery is unique in that the family does practically all the year round work, with only a little outside help during crush.

People in the Valley have long known that the product of this small, inconspicuous winery represents good value, for each year an already good product is made better. On many a festive table in the Valley, there proudly sits a bottle of Sutter's fine Zinfandel, or other wine, for Valley people are not particularly impressed with the size or modernity of a winery, but they definitely do respect the quality that leaves the bottle.

Across the street and down the road a way is a small tasting room that represents only the tip of a good sized iceberg. The sign says "Heitz Cellars" and many people, knowing that Heitz Cellars is a comparatively small winery, assume that this is it. In fact it was, until 1964, when Joe and his hardworking wife, Alice, bought the splendid old Rossi winery in Spring Valley which is the present site of their operations. The tasting room may be small, but a public getting progressively more sophisticated to wine flock to it, so that this small salesroom moves wine at a rate totally disproportionate to its small size.

At Galleron Road is the new, very modern Franciscan Winery which when it is in full operation will have a capacity of over 100,000 cases a year. The interior of this winery has bank after bank of stainless steel fermentors, a very advanced and rapid bottling line, and new oaken cooperage that rates with the finest in the Valley. One of the new ventures in the Valley, it is representative of the modern ideas that are causing considerable changes in a very ancient art.

Across the valley, on Taplin Road, Joseph Phelps, who came to the Valley from the construction business has built a winery that is a Valley showplace and an outstanding new addition to the list of fine wineries already here. Liberally endowed with the very finest of equipment including rectangular fiberglass tanks that are new to this valley, the winery will evoke much comment for the beauty of its architecture and the daring,

The Wine Library at Charles Krug Winery contains samples of the firm's best wines, dating back to 1943. Here, Peter Mondavi examines a fine old Cabernet from 1947, that is practically priceless. *Right:* This ninety foot tunnel, painstakingly hacked out of the sandstone by Chinese labor, today houses the fine wines of Spring Mountain Winery. The caves maintain a year round 58° temperature—perfect for aging or storing wines.

innovative concepts epitomized in the building. Redwood salvaged from a hundred year old bridge has been recycled and used as wall decorations for meeting rooms that set a new standard of opulence and subdued good taste. The new owner has already absorbed much of the Valley's feeling, for these beautiful rooms are open to the use of any qualified group.

The redwood winery occupies a knoll on what used to be the old Connolly Ranch, a cattle raising enterprise of some considerable size. There are 120 acres of newly planted vineyards within sight of the winery, and by 1976, these will furnish the grapes for the firm's estate bottlings. In the meantime, this winery will be a fine customer for any vineyardist who can meet winemaker Walter Schug's admittedly high standards.

Hidden away at the head of Taplin Road in a beautifully wooded hollow called Spring Valley, Joe Heitz crushes, ferments and ages the wines that have made him the most talked about winemaker since Andre Tschelistcheff, under whom Joe once worked. There are many beautiful old wine cellars in the Napa Valley, but Heitz Cellars is unique. The Italian who built it probably knew very little about architecture, but he had an innate love of beauty that expressed itself in a rhyolite stone building that is so perfectly proportioned, so well adapted to its purpose that it could hardly be surpassed today, even with all the conveniences modern science has provided us. The old building serves as an aging cellar now, and handsome well cared for oaken casks hold the priceless Cabernets and Chardonnays that have made Joe Heitz internationally famous as probably the best winemaker in America today . . . a statement which he vigorously denies. "Best" he points out, is a relative statement and depends on many factors, most of them variable and a matter of personal opinion. Nevertheless, he consistently turns out magnificent wines, and was the leader in the movement that moved Napa Valley wines out of the low or medium priced level to the higher priced status that their quality deserves and presently enjoys. It comes as some surprise to visitors that his small modern winery, housed in a hexagonal structure completed in 1972 can turn out, with equipment no different than anyone elses, wines that consistently come in at, or near the top, of the list in tastings that include the world's most prestigious and much better known wines.

Many firms located some miles from St. Helena nevertheless call this town home. Up on Pritchard Hill, on a site of breathtaking beauty, Donn Chappellet has built a distinctively different winery overlooking Lake Hennessey and much of the Napa Valley. Farther up the road, Jim Nichelini's winery, dating back to the turn of the century is the scene of weekend tastings that live on in story for years. While these people do not live within the city limits of St. Helena, they nevertheless feel that they are part of the community, and proudly claim the town as their own.

The varied background of the town is evident in its architecture, ranging from the cut stone buildings of the 1880's to California modern. There is a white needle-steepled Presbyterian church that is right out of New England, and a handsome, solidly built stone Catholic church that would be right at home in some affluent French wine country town. The Rhine house is blatantly Germanic, and in the sturdy if somewhat

Downtown St. Helena is an interesting blend of the old and the new. Note the stone construction of the old Masonic Hall. The larger rocks were used on the lower levels, the smaller at the higher. The local story is that the scaffolding got pretty wobbly as it got higher, so it wasn't trusted with too much weight. *Right:* A workman washes down fiberglass tanks at the Joseph Phelps winery on Taplin Road. These tanks, made in Germany, are new to the Valley, but will probably be soon seen in every winery since they are eminently practical.

narrow stone bridges that cross the Napa River, the influence of the Chinese laborers who built so many of the old buildings in St. Helena shows conspicuously. The old Italian cemetery is a vicarious trip to Tuscany, and almost everywhere, the Spanish heritage of this part of California is on full display. A casual ride through the streets of the town may lead to a home of obvious luxury, or take you by rows of modest homes that are nevertheless someone's well kept pride and joy.

The street lights along Main Street are probably as good a key to St. Helena's character as there is. Called "electroliers," these are cast iron relics of the 1915 Pan Pacific Exposition, and by modern lighting standards are painfully inefficient. They are also graceful, aesthetically pleasing, and blend beautifully with the general feeling of a town where a high efficiency sodium vapor lamp would be a jarringly false note.

Fortunately, the majority of its inhabitants recognize the values that make St. Helena so pleasant, and are militantly determined to preserve them, with the people recently arrived in town leading the fray. A recent survey showed that the town's undeniable charm was "very fragile" and susceptible to damage by even minor changes. For that reason, it gives the impression of being a place where time has somehow been arrested. More likely than not, that is exactly the reason why it is different . . . and desirable.

St. Helenans know a good thing when they experience it, so while they energetically make sure that their children will some day be able to experience the values that make this little town such a wonderful place to live, they also themselves enjoy it from day to day, and in so doing, count their blessings.

Franciscan Winery boasts of a very impressive array of stainless steel fermentors. This is the new look in wineries, replacing the older redwood tanks formerly used. *Right:* In 1883, Frederic Beringer commissioned a replica of his ancestral home in Mainz, Germany, to be erected in St. Helena. Beautifully restored, it today houses the tasting room and executive offices of the Beringer Brothers. *Pages 88-89:* On a knoll that is part of what formerly was the Connolly Ranch, the new Joseph Phelps winery sits comfortably amidst its vineyards. Built in 1973-74 this new winery is a valley showplace.

CHAPTER III

THAT RUTHERFORD DUST

The story is told that when Andre Tchelistcheff, the legendary winemaker of Beaulieu Vineyards was asked what was the critical ingredient in his outstanding Cabernets, he answered "Cabernets need a touch of that Rutherford dust." Tchelistcheff undoubtedly knows: he fermented some of the noblest wines ever produced in the Napa Valley, and people trained by him are carrying on that tradition, all with the aid of that Rutherford dust.

It is an undeniable fact that the Rutherford area imparts a distinctly different flavor to Cabernets, or for that matter, to any of the grapes grown in this region, for while the red wines have built the region's reputation, it also produces outstanding whites, all with that distinctive something the French call "gout de terre" (taste of the earth). There are knowledgeable tasters in the area who can pinpoint to within a hundred yards the place that produced the wine they are tasting. Apparently the geologic makeup of the Rutherford area is so distinctive and outstanding that its characteristics are imparted to a wine so emphatically that the trained palate can pick it out unerringly. It is only fair to point out that the Napa Valley has many extremely well trained palates, so don't bet against these individuals. You'd lose, as I did.

The Rutherford—Oakville area, geologically similar, is home to Inglenook Winery, built in 1884 by Gustave Niebaum, a Finnish sea captain turned viticulturist, and Beaulieu Vineyards which traces its beginning to 1900 when George de Latour, a young Frenchman with a love of beauty and wine, picked a beautiful spot ("Beau lieu" in French) in the valley for his home and vineyards. The gracious mansions they built as neighbors as well as friendly competitors still stand, and add considerably to the valley's social charm.

The Niebaum house, once occupied by Bud and Jean Van Loben Sels of Oakville Vineyards was and is a Valley showplace. Beautifully situated at the edge of the western mountains, it looks out over extensive vineyards that firmly established Inglenook's reputation as one of the world's finest wineries. The house, with its spacious verandas is a gem of Victorian architecture, with priceless wood paneling and stained glass, all of which was kept in perfect condition by the occupants' loving care. The Van Loben Sels family was very much aware that their beautiful home is a part of the Valley history, and were extremely generous in sharing it for civic and social functions. The Napa Valley Wine Library holds tastings there yearly, and somehow, the fragrant Napa Valley wines shared under those towering trees that shaded the legendary Captain Niebaum become even more tasty.

The de Latour home, now occupied by the builder's daughter, the Marquise de Pins, was placed at the end of a mile-long lane of flowering trees and featured extensive formal gardens. Like many of the early figures in the Napa Valley wine scene, George de Latour was a cultured man, a splendid host, equally at home with a corporation president or a vineyard worker, who lived the good life of the Napa Valley to the full. He felt personally involved with every bottle of wine that left his

Robert Mondavi, is certainly one of the most influential, talented and energetic winemakers in the Napa Valley. *Right:* The Mission-style buildings of the Robert Mondavi Winery flank Highway 29, near Oakville. Spacious lawns are the scene of summer jazz concerts, and provide a cool green island in a sea of vines. *Pages 92-93:* Following an Old World tradition, the first load of 1974 vintage grapes is blessed at the Robert Mondavi Winery. Usually the blessing is done by a Franciscan in deference to the large part that Order had in founding the wine industry in California, but this year the blessing was invoked by Father James Cleary, a popular Valley priest who is himself a vineyardist.

winery, which is probably the reason that during his own lifetime, he saw the name "Beaulieu" become synonymous with quality.

The Beaulieu Winery in Rutherford has recently been expanded by Heublein Inc., its new owner. A handsome new reception center serves as tasting room and shows an outstanding audio-visual report on the firm's wines. Rutherford Square, an adjacent enterprise that tastefully blends outdoor art with outdoor dining adds considerable charm to an already charming spot.

Beaulieu Vineyards and Inglenook are both owned by Heublein Inc. but function as separate entities and are strongly competitive. The original Inglenook Winery, built by Gustave Niebaum in 1884 was, and is, a Valley showplace. A long stone building with Georgian and Gothic overtones, it nestles at the bottom of the western foothills, as solid as the day it was built. The 1906 earthquake demolished many of the Valley's stone wineries, but Inglenook's vaulted stone cellars came through the catastrophic quake with only minor damages, and still can be admired today as perfect examples of how well the Valley's craftsmen built with stone. Well preserved oaken cooperage ages Inglenook's classic wines, and serves as a stellar tourist attraction. A feature of the noble old winery is the captain's room, panelled in fine woods and lighted by stained glass windows where Captain Niebaum's personally acquired drinking glasses and other artifacts are on display. Having a glass of good Inglenook wine in the captain's room is the supreme accolade a visitor to the old cellars can receive, and a privilege only very rarely granted.

Heublein's was well aware of the value of the Inglenook and Beaulieu names, for these two wineries have always stood for the very highest quality: a fact which has been affirmed by many gold medals received in competition with the world's most prestigious wines. The present line of wines, while offering a large selection of price ranges, does not neglect the very best. It is still possible to get Beaulieu and Inglenook reflecting the high ideals instituted by their distinguished founders.

A short way down the road is the Robert Mondavi Winery, completely surrounded by vineyards. Vaguely reminiscent of the Franciscan era of California architecture, it is actually an ultra modern, highly functional building crammed with the very latest centrifuges and traditional oak barrels. Probably better than any other winery in California, this one exemplifies a perfect marriage of modern technology and sound winemaking principles, and Bob Mondavi will be the first to tell you that this is exactly what he had in mind when he founded his business in 1966. A dynamic man exuding a restless energy, he has probably done as much as anyone to promote the virtues of California wine in general, and Napa Valley wine in particular. His elder son, Michael, is manager of the firm, and also a highly competent enologist who has inherited his father's drive and discriminating palate, qualities he shares with his younger brother, Tim, a recent graduate of U. C. Davis.

A unique feature of this winery is a large hall in the south wing where wine tastings, dinners, art exhibits and other functions are regularly held. Not surprisingly, this feature, The Vineyard Room, has made the Robert Mondavi winery a Valley social center. The large lawn behind the winery is also the scene of regularly sold out outdoor concerts in the summer. While this winery is

Small oak cooperage of 55 gallons capacity, stacked in tiers of thousands, hold the wine which Robert Mondavi Winery carefully ages until it has picked up just the right amount of oak flavor. *Right:* Inglenook Winery, built by Captain Gustave Niebaum, still operates today as a working winery. This beautiful building survived the great 1906 earthquake and Prohibition to keep intact the tradition of excellence it has enjoyed since its founding in 1884.

usually regarded as one of the best public relations oriented firms in the Valley its reputation rests solidly on the fact that it consistently produces outstandingly superior wine, and is leader in the research that constantly improves an already superlative product. There is an air of modern bustle and energy about this winery that is quite at variance with the slower tempo of older establishments, but no one can deny the virtue of what comes out of the bottles.

There is a popular misconception, usually fostered by wine writers enamoured of small family owned wineries, that great wine can be made only in small quantities, in quaint little stone cellars with a few old barrels and an antiquated basket press. This, of course, is nonsense, and no place refutes this fable more than the Robert Mondavi Winery. It is true that at his Oakville operation every help that modern technology has evolved is employed, but basically, this is only an improvement on the methods that have stood the test of time. Robert Mondavi is a firm believer in letting wine make itself, naturally, with only a little intelligent help here and there whenever the result is a better, more natural wine. For instance, this winery was the first to make extensive use of small oak cooperage, a practice now common in the industry. Everywhere, the emphasis is on making superlatively good wine even better, and no method whether ultra modern or traditional is ignored if it will achieve that end.

Only a few hundred yards down the road stands the flag bedecked tasting room and winery of Oakville Vineyards, which started life as the old Bartolucci Winery. Since 1969 it has been under the leadership of Wilfred Van Loben Sells who put together a limited partnership of almost 400 investors: an understandably hard core cadre of prime boosters. The winemaker is Peter Karl Becker, an affable ex-Luftwaffe pilot with some very firm ideas of how wines, especially whites, should be fermented and aged. Peter makes extensive use of centrifuges, in the German manner and ferments his white wines in stainless steel, eschewing the traditional oak aging. He believes this results in a fruity wine where the characteristics of the grape have not been overwhelmed by oak. "In vino veritas." That he is not alone in his opinion is evidenced by the fact that his wines have a large and growing following.

Through its associated partners and by outright ownership, Oakville vineyards controls over 1,000 acres, an enviable position for any winery. Part of the old Inglenook vineyards, whose grapes helped establish that winery's reputation are included in this ownership, so that this new winery has a heritage going back to the legendary Captain Niebaum. This diversity of vineyards has also made it possible for Oakville Vineyards to produce not only an excellent line of varietals sold under the Oakville and Van Loben Sels label, but also a reasonably priced line of house wines; red, white and rose, that are excellent in taste and value.

The Rutherford-Oakville region is relatively flat, but since it has an extremely varied mineral content; the legacy of mountain streams that deposited alluvial fans on the valley floor, it grows a wide variety of grapes. Some outstanding Cabernets are grown here, but it also produces Pinot Chardonnay, White Riesling, and a very distinctive French Colombard. On the Oakville Grade Road, Charles Krug has a small vineyard planted to the

Large redwood tanks, which impart no particular flavor to wine, are usually used for storage and aging of wines. These examples are at the Louis Martini Winery in St. Helena. *Right:* Perched high on the roof of the old Niebaum stables, a flicker surveys the lacework pattern which he and his kind have produced. Acorns will be placed in those holes. Then in a few days, the flicker returns and listens for noisy acorns. Those are the ones he will peck open, to get at the larvae living inside.

very delicate and much sought after Moscato Canelli, from which a sweet dessert wine is made that is always in short supply.

George de Latour and Captain Niebaum chose their winery sites primarily because of the grapes that could be grown there. Another man built here simply because of the beauty in which this region abounds. On a wooded knoll at the foot of the western mountains, David Doak, a millionaire industrialist poured millions into a brick Georgian mansion. Shrubs, statuary, and formal gardens made it the most grandiose setting in the Valley, but in spite of the millions spent on it, the Doak family found mostly tragedy there. It was finally acquired by Discalced Carmelites, who built a beautifully vaulted chapel on one end of the building, and transformed it into a monastery.

Now, silent, contemplative men walk in the beautiful gardens and a place built for a millionaire's pleasure has finally found peace in the hands of men vowed to poverty and silence. The chapel, open to the public, offers a cool serene solace that is always appreciated, but especially so on a hot summer day.

The eastern edge of the valley, especially near the Silverado Trail, is crowned by a series of rocky knolls of volcanic origin. In spite of difficulties attendant to building on such a site, these are favored building sites, and crowned by homes generally built by people to whom expense is only a minor consideration.

And all around them, the vineyards spread their rows, seasonably green and gold. The valley will not be denied: it is fulfilling its destiny, and growing its grapes to gladden the hearts of men.

The Captain's Room at Inglenook contains many artifacts personally used by Gustave Niebaum, who founded the winery. Here, by the light of a stained glass window, Brady McManus examines a fine Johannesberg Riesling. *Right:* In the cavernous depths of Inglenook Winery, huge old oaken cooperage hold a treasure of aging wines. These casks were assembled by skilled German craftsmen when the winery was built in 1884 and to this day age the noble wines of Inglenook. Note the stone ceiling, painstakingly cut stone by stone, and fitted so beautifully that these cellars suffered only very minor damage in the catastrophic 1906 quake that demolished buildings built with less attention to quality.

The Vineyard Room at Robert Mondavi Winery is in constant use as an Art Gallery, where contemporary artists can give their work a wide exposure. This facility serves thousands of people every year and is a valley social center. *Right:* At Oakville Vineyards, a bank of stainless steel fermentors flank the more traditional oaken casks. The piece of wheeled equipment in the foreground is a filtering unit used to free wine of suspended material.

CHAPTER IV

WHERE IT ALL BEGAN—YOUNTVILLE

Although Yountville is approximately at the halfway point in the Napa Valley, measured from Calistoga to San Pablo Bay, there are many people, especially in the upper valley who consider it the southern edge of the Napa Wine Country. This statement is icily denied by the many vineyardists who tend flourishing tracts south of Yountsville, and who are undeniably in the Napa Valley. It also seems an absurd statement to the growers in the Carneros region who raise many of the grapes on which the Napa Valley has built its reputation. There is also a winery at Carneros Creek, and another in Napa to say nothing of the vast plantings in the hills above the town. These are all a part of the complex that makes up the entity known as the Napa Wine Country.

There is, however, some justification for the feeling that Yountville somehow has its mind on something other than wine, in direct contrast to those towns to the north, where the emphasis is completely on things vinous. Yountville seems to be more preoccupied with its restored old buildings, its veteran's hospital and the tourist trade than it is with the industry which had its founding here. There is really nothing wrong with this, for Yountville prospers mightily on these wellsprings of its affluence. It does, however, add a certain touch of authenticity to the claim that the wine country proper begins just north of city limits.

While its inclusion in the wine country proper may be slightly debatable, there is no question at all about Yountville being an integral part of the over-all entity that is the Napa Valley, and a highly interesting, picturesque one at that. It was here that the pioneer George Yount built his mill and blockhouse, here that the first grapes in the Napa Valley were planted, and here that his remains are buried, in the valley he loved so well. The whole Napa Valley story as far as white occupancy is concerned, began here and its contributions to the Valley, past and present, can neither be denied nor denigrated.

Although the center of wine production has unquestionably shifted northward, it was not always thus. In 1890 Gottlieb Groezinger built a substantial brick winery in Yountville, and several smaller stone wineries flourished in the area. Yountville was a wine center, and the largest town in the North Valley. Its substantial brick and stone buildings show that it was an established center of commerce when St. Helena was just a scattered village. But while the northern part of the valley grew and prospered Yountville remained static. A large California State verteran's hospital situated to the west of town became the main focus of interest, and the town began to get that run-down look that always seems to accrue to communities that have run their span of life.

Then, the miracle happened and Yountville took on its second lease on life. The old Groezinger winery, scheduled for demolition, was bought by a group of investors who shrewdly guessed that it could be transformed into a stellar tourist attraction, and Vintage 1870 came into existence. The old brick winery's exterior was sandblasted, and the interior, kept as much as possible in its original shape, was transformed into

Since 1873, the Magnolia Hotel has been part of the Yountville scene. Recently renovated, it boasts four small but beautifully appointed rooms, a one entree menu . . . and a two weeks' waiting list! *Right:* Under a cloudy Spring sky, mustard blankets a field near the Yountville Crossroads and the Silverado Trail. *Pages 104-105:* Near the Carmelite Monastery, on the Oakville Grade, masses of acacia blossoms paint the February landscape with bright splashes of living gold.

a delightful maze of shops, restaurants, and boutiques. There is even a well attended playhouse.

Yountville has become a tourist mecca, in its own right worth a trip from the metropolitan centers of San Francisco and Oakland. The charmingly restored old stone Magnolia Hotel features a one entre meal, four diminutive rooms . . . and a two weeks' waiting list!

Yountville lies in a transitional zone just about at the dividing line between the Maritime Zone, strongly in-fluenced by the fogs emanating from San Pablo Bay and the warmer Coastal Zone which extends approximately to St. Helena. It is thus better suited to the Pinot Noir variety of red grape, rather than the Cabernet, which thrives on more heat and many of the distinguished Pinot Noir vintages of the Valley originate in this area. It also grows a distinctive White Riesling the source of some of the Valley's most distinguished Johannisberg Rieslings. As in all the rest of the Valley, the geological composition of the soil varies from place to place, so that a 100 acre plot can easily be planted to three dif-ferent varieties each one occupying the place most suitable to its development. This geological difference is not only detectable on the ground by soil analysis, but is actually visible from the air. The alluvial fans can be seen as variously shaded deposits, each with its own growing characteristics. Little by little these de-posits are being pinpointed and identified, so that the best possible use may be made of their peculiar virtues.

It should be remembered that it took centuries of trial and error to correctly identify those spots in French vineyards that would produce the ultimate grape. The process is less than one hundred years old in the Napa Valley, and while applied technology is an extremely valuable tool, the ultimate test is still the quality of the

Half the fun of buying a bottle of wine is talking about it, as here at Groezingers, in the Vintage 1870 complex at Yountville. *Right:* in a quiet cemetery in Yountville, a marble memorial shaft marks the grave of George C. Yount, the Napa Valley pioneer white settler. Within sight is a better living memorial: the vineyards he planted, which first demonstrated to the world the qualities that were to make the Valley famous as a premier winegrow-ing region. *Pages 108-109:* Autumn brings a blaze of color to the Valley. Red wine grape leaves turn red, white wine grape leaves turn gold. Here, a Petite Sirah vine glows with the last flush of autumn.

wine that is actually produced from that plot, and that takes time, sometimes even generations. Some plots in the Napa Valley have been planted to three or more varieties, and the search still goes on to find the variety that will produce supreme quality in any one spot.

When George Yount first planted his Mission grape in the Yountville area, he was undoubtedly pleased to see the rich, full clusters the virgin soil produced. He probably would be astounded to learn today that the Mission grape has practically disappeared from the Napa Valley, supplanted by better, if not more prolific varieties.

The Veteran's Hospital at Yountville, a facility of the State of California has had a stabilizing effect on the economy of the town, since it is always there, in good times as well as bad. It is actually a self-contained town, but, as in all such establishments, even one as beautifully situated and equipped as this one, there is always a desire to get away, so that downtown Yountville has a preponderance of single men, and of cross streets marked "Veterans' Crossing."

Yountville may not be as completely wine oriented as are the towns in the northern part of the Valley, but it is inevitably influenced by the vineyards and wineries at its doorstep. All the restaurants have a good wine list, and expert wine tasters abound. Many of the people who work in the Oakville-Rutherford, and even St. Helena area live in Yountville, finding there a way of life that suits them completely.

Evidently, the charm that made George Yount perfectly content to live out his days in this spot still works, for to several thousand perfectly contented people this is the most beautiful spot in California: their joy, their pride, their home.

A festive setting—a holiday turkey and a bottle of good Napa Valley wine to complement it. *Right:* Near Yountville, a hundred year old Victorian mansion sits in a field yellow with the mustard of Spring.

The Lincoln house, one of the oldest pioneer homes in the Valley, sits comfortably in the midst of its vineyards. The house has been used for movie and TV settings, is over 100 years old, and is charmingly furnished with period furniture. *Right:* Dating back to 1895 the buildings of Freemark Abbey house not only the winery of that name, but also a restaurant, gift shop, and nationally famous candle factory.

CHAPTER V

BROTHER TIM'S VINEYARD

Any region that is sufficiently different that it produces its own characteristic way of life is bound to have people who epitomize that style. The Napa Valley is no exception, except that its style of life is so complex and varied, depending on who lives it that it would be practically impossible to pick out any one person and say "This person represents the best in the Napa Valley."

Any such contest would most likely narrow down to two or at most three contestants. One of these would certainly be Brother Timothy F.S.C. the legendary cellarmaster of the Christian Brothers.

It comes as quite a surprise to many people to find that there really is a Brother Timothy, and that he actually is the boss of wine operations at Christian Brothers. Make no mistake about it: Brother Tim is very much alive and well in the hills above Napa Valley, and while he may belittle his own importance, and point out that he has a superior whose orders he follows, nevertheless, his views have a habit of becoming company policy. The fact that under his aegis the Christian Brothers have become the largest producers in the Napa Valley, and that the wines he ferments have acquired an enviable position for consistent quality speak for the validity of this kindly man's judgment and ability.

The Christian Brothers are a world-wide teaching order of the Roman Catholic Church founded in 1680 in Rheims, France, by St. Jean Baptiste de La Salle. It is an order of laymen who have taken vows of poverty, chastity, and obedience. Although primarily a teaching order, they made wine in their former location in Martinez, California. In 1930, during the Depression, they moved their operation to a wooded hillside on Redwood Road, eight miles above Napa, where in 1903 Theo. Gier had built a substantial stone winery. This location became the hub not only of their wine making operations, but also of their novitiate and boarding school. The beautiful hillside vineyards were expanded and replanted, and the Brothers began to quietly build up a following for their wine.

The success of any business venture is largely predicated on having the right man take charge at the right time. And in Brother John F.S.C. who headed the venture until his death in 1962, the Brothers found the right man. Brother John was an extremely astute businessman with an uncanny ability when it came to picking people to work with him. Not the least of his appointments was that of Brother Timothy, who has been involved in the wine operations since 1935.

"That's quite a time to work for the same outfit without a raise!" he'll tell you with a twinkle in his hazel eyes.

The Brothers' operations soon outgrew the Mt. La Salle location, so in 1950 they acquired the Greystone cellars on the northern outskirts of St. Helena. This imposing stone building, not only houses most of their aging wines, but also serves as the plant for the Charmat process champagne that has contributed not a little to the Brothers' reputation for turning out a superior product at a reasonable price. On the southern

These two corkscrews, from Brother Timothy's collection, are Prohibition era caricatures of Senator Volstead, nicknamed "Old Snifter". The Senator was, understandably, not exactly popular in the Napa Valley. *Right:* The man, and his life work, are epitomized in this picture of Brother Timothy, F.S.C., the cellarmaster of the Christian Brothers, examining a cluster of white wine grapes in the mountain vineyards of Mt. La Salle; the buildings of which are shown in the background.

edge of St. Helena, they have an ultra modern complex of crushers, continuous process presses and stainless steel fermentors that is as modern and efficient as any in the industry. This is the hub of a planned complex that will eventually perform the greater part of the Brothers' operations in the valley, while Mt. La Salle will remain an attractively situated aging cellar and tasting room with only minor production facilities.

Of all the producers in the Valley, the Christian Brothers is the only one that does not produce a vintage dated varietal. Brother Tim explained this to me one afternoon over a glass of excellent Johannisberg Riesling.

The reason they do not date their varietals is that they prefer the freedom that comes with blending and are willing to pay the price of operating without vintage dating to achieve that end. Whatever vintage year is necessary to bring the best characteristic to the wine being made can be provided, and the resulting blend is not only a very fine and complex wine, but also one with a guaranteed continuity of quality.

"We want to assure our customers that when they buy a bottle of Christian Brothers' wine, they are buying something with which they are familiar and which is something they'll be able to buy next year."

The Brothers' stock of wine is very extensive, dating back to many superlative vintages, and these are the wines that find their way into the bottles sold under the Christian Brothers label. Each wine is carefully evaluated, both for its strong and weak points, and the necessary compensating wine is added to the blend, each one adding something to the whole, so that the blend is an improvement over any one of its component parts.

Of course, the success of a blend depends very strong-

The hands of Brother Timothy gently cradle a cluster of grapes, before he cuts the stem. Constant vigilance is the price, not only of freedom, but also of a healthy vineyard. *Right:* The mustard of early Spring paints the slopes of Mt. La Salle's mountain vineyards with a splash of brilliant yellow.

ly on the skill and palate of the blendor, and Brother Tim is very proud that in Leonard "Bud" Berg they have a supremely good taster and blender. And yet, when you hear these words from this tall, ruddy-faced, gentle man, you get the idea that although many people have a hand in the blending, the final step is still the master of the cellar, and that is undeniably Brother Tim.

In the field of blending, which is actually done by most of the valley's producers, the Christian Brothers have one outstanding advantage. Their vineyards are so extensive, so scattered over the whole Valley that they have wines of all the varied characteristics the Valley produces, and the storage space to let them age properly. They can keep wines for years, if that is necessary, and some of those old stored Pinot Noirs and Cabernets must be priceless by now. They certainly do not decry the value of a varietal from any one year— they are the first to admit that this can be an exceptional wine. However, as a large producer who must turn out an unvariably good product every year, they believe that this is best achieved by blending. The fact that the showcases at Mt. La Salle and Greystone are heavy with gold and silver medals won in state and international competitions would seem to indicate that very many people, customers and judges alike, agree with them.

One of the characteristics of vintners in the Napa Valley that really impresses anyone from elsewhere is the spirit of friendliness and mutual help that is so evident on all sides. Time after time, as I researched materials for this book, I was told of instances of help freely given and received, not as an exceptional occurrence, but as a simple day to day happening. You had a

Brother Timothy's corkscrew collection is so famous that when he contacted a collector's group in London, they voted him to be the head man, with the title of "Right", because, they said, "any American would rather be Right than President". *Right:* Painstakingly coopered by skilled German craftsmen, the ancient casks of Greystone to this day mellow and age the choice wines of the Christian Brothers. *Pages 120-121:* The slopes near Mount La Salle glow with crimson and gold in a late autumn day.

breakdown? A phone call to anyone of a dozen of your competitors will bring either the equipment needed or help in finding it. Run into a problem that takes some expert advice? That's the most freely given of all commodities, and usually practical, workable advice at that. Bob Trinchero, of Sutter's Home Winery lists as one of the big advantages of his winery's location the fact that it is just across the road from Louis Martini.

"If Louis doesn't know the answer, the problem isn't important anyway," he tells you, in all dead seriousness.

It's a way of life in the Napa Valley, and time after time as these instances are related, Brother Tim figures in them. Small wonder that he is held in such high esteem by all his competitors.

"You know," one of them told me, "I always see a halo atop a bottle of Christian Brothers wine, and I figure that halo's worth about fifty cents!"

A tour through the cool cellars of Mt. La Salle is a treat any time, but especially so after Brother Tim has taken you for a tour, part of it perpendicular through his beloved vineyards. This cultured, intelligent man has a feeling for soil, for vines, and for people, and nowhere is it more apparent then when he is in one of his hillside vineyards, and lets his eyes roam fondly over acres of lovingly tended vines. Somehow he seems to sum up in his own person the words that formerly graced the back label of each bottle of Christian Brothers wine. "High in the hills above the Napa Valley, the Christian Brothers practice the ancient art of the vintner, and gladden the heart of man."

Bless you, Brother, may you live forever!

Brother Timothy in his favorite spot . . . the vineyards entrusted to his care. *Right:* The second floor of Greystone houses part of Brother Timothy's extensive collection of corkscrews, as well as a few antique basket presses (no longer in use) and old casks which very definitely are still used. *Pages 124-125:* Completed in 1889, this is the world's largest stone winery. Named "Greystone," it is an aging cellar for the Christian Brothers store of fine old wines, and also houses their Charmat process champagne facilities.

High in the mountains above the Napa Valley, on Redwood Road, the church and school buildings of Mt. La Salle rise amidst the mountain vineyards that have established an enviable reputation for the Christian Brothers. *Left:* Holy Family Church in Rutherford has, since 1912, served the spiritual needs of the area's numerous Roman Catholics. After Mass, people gather, talk, renew old friendships and generally make it a pleasant social occasion. *Page 128:* The Cabernet Sauvignon is the noble grape from which the finest red Bordeaux wines are made. In the Napa Valley this grape is often made into a 100% varietal wine that wins praise from wine connoisseurs all over the world, and especially from the chauvinistic, but knowledgeable French wine drinkers. *Page 129:* The White Riesling grape, which is the basis of the great Johannisberger Rieslings of Germany, produces in the Napa Valley, a fruity, semi-sweet wine that is probably the most popular of all the white table wines produced in this country.

The beautifully kept lawns of Charles Krug are the scenes of numerous concerts and social gatherings. This is the oldest winery in the Napa Valley, dating back to 1861. *Right:* In the Spring new vine shoots must be tied into correct growing position, a job which provides spending money for a considerable portion of the Valley's youth.

CHAPTER VI

THE LURE OF THE HILLSIDES

With most people, established habits, especially those sanctioned by centuries of tradition, are hard to break, so it was predictable that when a vineyardist arrived from the Old World, he would bring with him the ideas and habits inherited from his ancestors. Centuries of tradition and sound practice dictated that he should plant his vines on a hillside versus a plain. It had always been thus, in the Old Country. Plains were reserved for food grains and truck gardens; vines would thrive on poor soil that would cause the hardiest grains to wilt.

It is true that some vines seem to produce their best fruit when planted in "poor soil." That soil may be "poor" simply because of a deficiency of minerals that may provide too weak a diet for, say, a carrot, but is perfectly suited to the needs of a Cabernet. Vines will also thrive in rich soil, and produce heavy, beautiful clusters that seldom have the character of that produced by a vine that has experienced some suffering.

In the Napa Valley, this doesn't always hold true. The Valley floor is largely composed of alluvial fans washed down from the surrounding heights, so the level ground offers all the advantages of the minerals in the mountain terrain, plus a level place on which to work, and which also greatly facilitates the movement of the machinery that has so largely supplanted the heavy labor formerly done by hand.

The early European settlers sought the hills. Schramsberg's reputation for fine wine was founded on the hillside vineyards Jacob Schram so painfully wrested from the forest. His journals recall that the product of his mountain vineyards were the "superior" grapes and that he would mix their somewhat meager output with "inferior" valley grapes only with the greatest reluctance.

All through the hills surrounding the Valley, there are remnants of old vineyards and the wineries built there to utilize their production. It must be admitted that there are many factors in favor of a mountainous site, some of which are still pertinent, while others have lost their relevance in the light of modern technology.

As has been stated before, many hillside vineyards were established simply because that was the established norm. This system did have some advantages. Once the vines were well rooted (and that took some back-breaking water carrying to accomplish), they thrived in well-drained soil, since the roots of an established vine easily goes down ten feet for moisture. The hills generally have more Spring rain than the flatlands, and drain it off faster. A rocky hillside will hold the heat of the sun for some hours after sunset, and so hasten the process of ripening. Also, as has been stated before, the mineral content of a mountainous site could give a grape a flavor and complexity that could be achieved in the valley only if grapes were planted in soil that had been washed down from that same elevation.

The big thing in favor of a mountain vineyard, though, was simply that grapes planted at an elevation were much less susceptible to frost damage during the critical days of new vine growth. A mountain vineyard could always be counted on to produce a crop: meager, perhaps, compared to the lush yields of the valley floor, but nevertheless consistently producing. That virtue

The bladder press is the workhorse of the industry. Fermented pomace is dumped into the perforated steel cage and hydraulic pressure exerted through a polyethylene tube presses out the remaining wine. Not nearly as picturesque as the old basket press, but much more efficient. *Right:* Donn Chappellet's mountain top winery holds many barrels of Cabernet Sauvignon, housed in a building partly buried in the earth, and shaped like a gigantic triangle. This is a very modern, and often copied concept.

alone makes mountain vineyards desirable, and it is no wonder that the hills around the Napa Valley still boast of many actively producing units.

Modern methods of frost protection have diminished the frost danger, and the advantages of a mountain vineyard are mostly offset by the disadvantages they present to mechanized farming. If a vineyardist can get a good stretch of flat land, especially on an alluvial fan washed down from the mountains, he will usually prefer that to a mountainous setting. The big problem is that such land is very limited and probably already in grapes thus zealously guarded by an owner aware of its value.

In spite of the problems attendant to their cultivation, mountain vineyards are still very highly prized. The 90 acres of Jerry Draper's mountain vineyard, crowned by an authentic-looking French provincial chateau, are probably the most valuable acres, from the standpoint of quality, in the United States. Louis Martini, who owns many hundreds of producing acres rates his Monto Rosso vineyard as his crowning jewel.

There is some kind of geological deposit at the 1200 foot level, starting from Diamond Mountain near Calistoga to a point seven miles north of Napa, the vicinity of Mt. La Salle, that fosters premium quality grapes, for this belt contains some of the best growing areas in the United States. Fans emanating from this deposit have the same characteristics, and grow grapes that have solidly established the Napa Valley wines' reputation for excellence. It also accounts for the fact that the larger vineyards in the Valley are on the west side. The eastern side has a similar deposit, but it doesn't reach as high, and since there are fewer creeks from this side, has a much smaller alluvial fan system. Still, Souverain, Cuvaison, Chappelet and Stag's Leap all feed from this, and Nathan Fay's excellent vineyard is dependent upon the minerals in it.

Up on Pritchard Hill, on a beautiful mountain site overlooking Lake Hennessy, Donn and Molly Chappellet have taken advantage of this phenomenon and are growing some of the best grapes in the region, which they transform into superb wines in a modernistic triangular roofed winery which is a veritable temple to Bacchus. The distinctive flavor of these wines, which has won universal acclaim, is at least in part attributable to the soil that produced them, and there is no soil exactly like it anywhere else.

On the same side of the valley, up on Howell Mountain, Tom and Linda Burgess have one of the most spectacularly beautiful views in the valley, right from their living room window. It isn't only a beautiful home and view: the mountainside-vineyards produce a Cabernet and Zinfandel of exceptional quality, which Tom proudly bottles under the name of Burgess Cellars.

Near the top of Veeder Mountain, Bob and Nonie Travers plant their vines in the crater of an extinct volcano and produce a prize winning Chardonnay that is pure liquid gold. Farther down the mountain, Mike and Arlene Bernstein tend their newly planted Cabernets and look forward to the next harvest when the hard work they have put into their fledgling vineyard and winery will be rewarded.

Life is hard on the mountains, but it also is tremendously rewarding, paying off as it does in a set of values that could not be even appreciated by those unaccustomed to the heady atmosphere of the heights.

A picker at Chateau Montelena ignores the camera and busily picks his way through the lush Zinfandel vines. *Right:* The old wall dates back to the 1890's, at Burgess Cellars, but the cooperage is new, and the vigilant cellarmaster is a young man; part of the new breed that are carrying on a proud tradition. *Pages 136-137:* Day dies beautifully in the Napa Valley, especially if one is lucky enough to view sunset on the way down from Pritchard Hill, with Lake Hennessey in the middle foreground.

CHAPTER VII

DE LATOUR, MONDAVI, VALLEJO, AND HEITZ

People who have travelled extensively in Europe are usually the first to notice that in many ways the Napa Valley resembles some of the more delightful parts of that continent. The climate is reminiscent of Cote D'Or, and the oaks and occasional scattered palms in the Valley give the landscape a decidedly Mediterranean look. A Frenchman, Italian or Spaniard would feel right at home here, because there are so many things that would remind him of his native land, and that may be the reason why the region's roots strike so deeply into those countries.

Something other than similarity to native climate would have to explain the reason why so many Germans emigrated to the Valley, and thrived mightily there. The 1860's and 1870's saw a mild migration of Germans to the Valley, and while some of them, like Charles Krug, Jacob Schram and the Beringer Brothers grew to be respected winery owners, the majority of them left their mark in the skilled crafts they plied in their new home. Skilled German craftsmen built the Rhine House, and some of them stayed in the Valley to embellish other homes with the fruit of their skills and labors. The carved oaken heads of casks and barrels in Greystone, Inglenook and Beringer's tunnels show a decidedly Germanic flair, and more likely than not, were carved by men who had learned their trade in Germany.

The Germans also brought their skill, diligence, and discipline in the making of white wine to the Valley. While the grapes grown here are more adapted to the methods common in French vineyards, and most wines are made following the guidelines layed down by French winemakrers, there are distinctly Germanic touches here and there, especially in the care and finishing of the Riesling wines. The latter day emigrants from Germany, and the winemakers of German origin distinctly show preferences in their methods that can easily be attributed to their Germanic forebears.

Hanns Kornell prefers the Riesling type grape—a German import—for his excellent champagne, as opposed to his good friend, Jack Davies, who favors French origin grapes. Hanns also brings to his business typically Germanic traits: hard work, attention to detail, and a blunt honesty that is sometimes somewhat disconcerting to those accustomed to a less direct method of address.

When Sterling Vineyards had completed their new buildings on a knoll overlooking Hanns' Larkmead Lane winery, they gave an appreciation dinner for the Valley's winery owners who had so liberally helped them during the construction of the beautiful new buildings, which to most people looks like a Greek monastery crowning some island in the Aegean Sea. Not to Hanns. When his turn came for a few comments, after the well earned complimentary remarks, he said:

"I vas very glad to find, coming up here, that you were really building a vinery. From Larkmead Lane it looks like gun emplacements. That's one way to get rid of the competition."

Another winemaker with Germanic forebears is Joe Heitz, who although he was born in Illinois, brings to the Napa Valley the same attention to detail and blunt

From time immemorial, workers in the vineyards have balanced loads on their head. Here a Mexican picker at Chateau Montelena heads for the gondola with a forty pound load. *Right:* At Stony Hill winery a basket-press, under pressure, spurts forth the juice of the mountain grown Chardonnay, which has established a national reputation for this tiny winery. Only very small wineries, such as this one, still use the basket presses, although it formerly was the workhorse of the industry. Pages 140-141: The Napa Valley has been called "the Great Unfenced Park". This scene is just off the Oakville Crossroads, near the Silverado Trail.

honesty that have made Hanns Kornell a legend. A tour of the spotlessly clean Heitz Cellars, and the methodical, precise methods he brings to his winemaking shows immediately that he comes from a race that not only values these qualities, but makes them a way of life. Joe's forthright appreciation of good food and wine, his generous hospitality, and his knowledge that hard work is the key to achievement also smacks mightily of the Germanic, for while this race has no monopoly on these qualities, it has certainly made them a hallmark.

Joe makes wines of unquestioned excellence, and has been referred to by many responsible publications as "probably the best winemaker in the United States." There is no question whatsoever that he would be a leading contender for that title. The wines he makes all have a distinctly different nose and flavor, that to the initiated immediately identifies their origin. Asked about this he simply answers:

"There's a bit of me in every bottle. I guess I just smell different."

As could be expected, the French have left their distinctive cachet on the Valley, for no region that could produce wine like this would long escape their attention. French grapes, French methods, French traditions inevitably attracted Frenchmen, who found here conditions so ideal for growing the grapes of their native lands that even these usually unshakable chauvinists began to admit that this region was a distinct challenge to their beloved Bordeaux and Burgundy. The Frenchman's love for the soil found fertile ground here; for this was soil rivaling even that of the best French vineyards, and there was no need of organic fertilizer in this virgin, undepleted land.

The most distinctly French winery in the Napa Valley was Beaulieu Vineyards founded in 1900 by George de Latour. While he began this winery as a comparatively poor man, the excellence of the wine he made at Beaulieu soon enabled him and his charming wife, Fernande, to live the lives of the French seigneurs to which nature and their heritage had inclined them. The fact that they did this so easily in the Napa Valley indicates how European the outlook had become. The constant stream of Europeans had completely transformed the social structure so that Napa Valley had become a small transplanted part of the European way of life . . . albeit with a distinctly American accent.

Today the French influence is still very strong, and is evident on all sides. Many of the wineries sport good American names: Chappellet, Beaulieu, Cuvaison, Chateau Chevalier, Chateau Montelena, with obviously French roots. There are several authentically French restaurants in the Valley, the local winemakers speak knowledgeably of French vintages, and have the better ones in their cellars. The sons of French "vignerons" spend the summer in the Napa Valley studying local winemaking methods, then return to France in the Fall taking with them as guests the sons of Valley winemakers. French is a good second language to have in the Napa Valley.

A large, recently opened operation in the Napa Valley speaks more eloquently than anything else about French opinion of the local wines. Moet-Hennessy, the French champagne and cognac firm, has opened a large new plant near Castle Rock feeding off 600 acres of choice Napa Valley hillside vineyards, and intends to

Napa Valley vintners not only drink their own and their neighbors' wine, but also have extensive cellars of the best imported vintages. This bin is in Don Chappellet's excellent cellar. *Right:* As would be expected from a winery that produces such superlative wine, Joe Heitz's aging cellar is spotless. The large table is often used for large group dinners, which are enhanced by a touch not often found in wineries; chandeliers which Joe rescued from an old house scheduled for demolition.

market the wines produced in the United States and part of them also eventually in France, although there, by law it may not be called champagne. A Frenchman investing his hard-earned francs in a foreign vineyard is paying it the supreme accolade.

Important as the German and French influence is in the Valley, they are nevertheless secondary to the Italian, which presently is indubitably the dominant way of life. The Italians were a little late into getting into the Valley, but what they lost in tardiness, they made up in numbers. In the 1880's and 1890's the bulk of the new arrivals were men who had a consuming love of the soil, a lust for life, a knack for making good wine . . . and Italian names.

The Italians came from all sections of Italy, but the North Italians seemed to feel most at home in this Valley, while the South Italians preferred the hotter San Joaquin area. Most of the smaller wineries that date from this period, were built by Italians with the help of Chinese hand labor, and the fact that most of the wineries are still in use proves that they built extremely well. The Italian love of the beautiful is evident in these buildings, for while they were functional they also achieved that simple beauty which comes so naturally to these gifted people.

The Italian influence became very strong in the decade before Prohibition, although most Italian producers made a comparatively simple, strong wine, rather than the more aristocratic complex vintages of Beaulieu and Inglenook. This stemmed mostly from the Italian philosophy that wine is something that should always be consumed with food, and not used primarily as a beverage, although this theory got strained a bit during Prohibition, when conditions made the beverage so precious that its consumption was not always attended with all the social amenities. The Italians also could not believe that such an unnatural law could last very long, so they had a tendency to hang on to their vineyards long after the others had given up and planted them to prunes. When the national madness finally subsided they were ready, willing and able to resume the trade that they had never really forsaken.

The post Prohibition era was a time of turmoil in the Valley, with wineries springing up overnight to help slake the great thirst. Many of these made very bad wine. They either did not survive or were forced to mend their ways as the consuming public became more sophisticated and good wine became available. But some of the giants of the industry date from this period.

A new breed of winemakers with Italian sounding names also came onto the scene. Those, however, were second generation, college educated Americans, and they brought with them a new philosophy. Led by men like Louis P. Martini, Bob and Peter Mondavi, Bruno Solari and Bob Trinchero the industry took a new twist. Gone or minimized, was the jug wine of yesterday. The emphasis was to be on quality and varietal wines.

This brings us up to the present day.

Three of the large wineries in the Napa Valley are owned by people of Italian descent; as well as numerous smaller ones. But the greater contributions that Italians have made are not as tangible as brick and mortar. The biggest contribution the Italians have made to the Napa Valley is their love of hard work, laughter, and joy of living. The Valley lives an Italianate way of life,

The Cabernet Sauvignon is characterized by a loose, open cluster, and light yield. In the Napa Valley it yields a wine quite different from that produced in Bordeaux, but which has thousands of ardent devotees. *Right:* The famed Beringer caves have been refurbished and serve not only as a repository for aging wines, but as a tourist attraction that draws hundreds of thousands of visitors every year.

and great as other achievements may be, they take second place to this joyous legacy.

The Spanish influence is strong everywhere in Central and Southern California, and the Napa Valley has not escaped it. The flag of Mexico once flew over this territory, and those early beginnings left indelible marks in the character of the Valley. General Mario Vallejo's Mexican land grant took in most of the Valley, and George Yount, though born in North Carolina, became a Mexican citizen in order to qualify for his own grant. It was inevitable that the contiguity of California and Mexico should result in some melding of the two cultures, and the results definitely show in the Valley.

One of the early showplaces of the Valley was the Parrot house, the home of Tiburcio Parrot, an aristocrat of the first water who wore his Castilian blood as a badge of honor. He and Frederic Beringer not only were fast friends, but the social arbiters of their day; and the sight of Senor Parrot and his lovely wife approaching the Rhine House in their splendid carriage, complete with liveried footmen, was one of the social highlights of early St. Helena.

All through the Valley, to this day, Mexican land grants form the basis of ownership for many famous vineyards. Although the landed aristocracy has long since been supplanted or assimilated, vestiges of their gracious way of life, their architecture, even their cooking persist to this day, and help to give the Valley its particular flavor.

The first vineyard workers in the Valley were Indians, but they succumbed rather easily to the white man's diseases. In their place, to fill the vacuum, came the Chinese, then later Mexicans and Spanish-Americans who quickly demonstrated a marked ability for this work. Today, a large part of the manual labor in the Valley is done by Mexican nationals, many of them admittedly in this country by virtue of a clandestine crossing of the Rio Grande, who prune the vines, trellis the canes, and harvest the grapes. The work is some-

In the Rhine House, built for Frederic Beringer in 1883, stained glass windows enhance the Old World appearance of this beautiful old mansion. *Right:* The old Rossi winery, built in 1890, is now the aging cellars for Joe Heitz's fine wines. Built of rhyolite quarried on the property, it is a superb example of those old Italians' genius with stone.

times cold and wet, often monotonous, and during harvest, hot and demanding. Yet the work is done to a constant stream of banter, and even song. An unforgettable memory for me was to hear a bronzed, stubble-faced grape cutter with a magnificent tenor voice flawlessly render Rudolfo's aria "Che gelida manina" from "La Boheme," and still manage to cut an impressive amount of grapes. I've payed good money to hear it done in a lesser manner, and certainly have never enjoyed it more, especially since the setting and source were so improbable.

There has been much social agitation aimed at the grape industry because of alleged exploitation of "these poor, ignorant people," mostly by earnest urban do-goods who have never met one of these men. One of "these poor ignorant people" I talked to spoke five languages — fluently — was studying law, and made enough money in three months of admittedly hard work to live quite comfortably the rest of the year in Mexico. He was also willing to do work that would find few or no takers in a nation where most of the stoop labor is considered below a man's dignity, and where dedication seems to be the idea that more pay should be paid for less work, blithely ignoring the economics involved. Whatever the argument, the point is that these men were doing a hard, useful labor, and doing it with the dignity that is the hallmark of a proud people.

Another ethnic group has left its indelible mark on the Valley. Everywhere, stone walls were built by clearing the land of rocks and piling them into neat rows marking the field's boundaries. The Chinese came to California during the gold rush, which happened to coincide with a time when China was torn by an internecine feud that took twenty million lives. Often despised, persecuted, and exploited, they somehow managed to survive and left behind striking monuments to their genius. A people that could build the Great Wall of China may not have found much challenge in building a five foot stone wall, but they built it with pride

The ranch foreman is an integral part of the system that gets the grapes off the vine and into the crusher. He is the boss, and usually a man who has done every one of the jobs that he supervises. When he shows a new worker how to do a job, he speaks from a position of authority. He knows! *Right:* Bottle recycling is not a new idea, as this old rack outside the Heitz Cellars winery will attest. Back in the 1890's, wine was bottled in almost any available container, and this rack drained the bottles that had been washed preparatory to filling with wine.

and expertise. They also excavated the tunnels of Beringer, Schramsberg and Stag's Leap, patiently hacking out the sandstone with pick and shovel and carrying out the detritus in baskets. Most of the stone wineries in the Valley were built with their help, and the sturdy stone bridges they erected spanning the Napa River probably will last as long as there is a need for them. Those patient, skilled, self-effacing people left their mark on the Valley, and it is a better place because they passed this way.

America has always drawn its hybrid vigor from the myriad complex of nationalities that have made this country home, and who are all, proudly, Americans, however their name may be rooted in other countries. Andre Tschelistcheff is a good American born in Russia who speaks English with a French accent and French with a Russian accent. Mike Grgich is a good American whose Croatian accent is almost as fruity as his Johannisberg Riesling. Hanns Kornell is a perfervid American whose patriotism expresses the intense appreciation and love he has for this, his adopted country. The Valley is studded with names that have their roots in France, Germany, England, Scotland, Denmark, Mexico, Holland, or almost any country you might name, each one bringing to the Valley his little touch that makes it a better place to live. Maybe it is a measure of that love each one has for this beautiful place that they each bring their best trait, and so help to make a good way of life even better.

The Valley's cultural and ethnic heritage is rich and varied, a legacy of the many people who have lived here, and left the best of their heritage behind. It is probably for that reason that when Michael Loesser wanted a setting for his prophetically named "The Most Happy Fella," he placed him here, in the Napa Valley.

The choice was apt. Happiness comes easily here, as a natural consequence of living in the Valley.

As kids will do, anyplace where there is water over knee-deep, youngsters congregate at the popular swimming hole on the Napa River below Lodi Lane. *Right:* Young vines, trained in the manner of the Rheingau, form a pattern of living young green in the spring. Note the presence of small stones, desirable in a vineyard because it assures good drainage and a high degree of heat retention. *Pages 152-153:* The automated warehouse at Inglenook's new installation in Rutherford is computer operated and completely modern. This view, taken from a lift truck, gives some idea of the capacity this new warehouse achieves.

CHAPTER VIII

THE QUIET TIME — WINTER

The November rains finally come, and the newly fermented wines are consigned to their aging casks to begin the long sleep that will convey to them the nobility to which they were born. The fields, bereft of their harvest robes of purple and gold, stand ghostly in gray, serried ranks, the gnarled arms of the vines grotesquely reaching to the heavens in silent supplication. The winter season has come to the Napa Valley.

Although the Fall rains bring a bright coat of newly sprouted grass, this is the season when there is the least apparent life in a vineyard. After their hard struggle, the vines having borne fruit rest and begin to recoup their strength, so that they may produce again, and keep intact nature's eternal cycle. Nutrient is stored, and although the plant goes into a state of dormancy that simulates death, it is undergoing a process that is an essential step in the complicated cycle that will produce another abundant crop next October.

Winter is the vineyardist's least busy time, but not the cellarman's. While the vineyardist waits for Spring to awaken the vines so that he may again nurture them, the cellarman is busy with the last vintage. New wines must be racked, some wines must be fined and transferred from tank to tank. Vintages that have come of age must be bottled and stored, and the emptied tanks cleaned. A winery takes a lot of housecleaning, and much of it is done in Winter, the quiet time.

Dormancy is an important part of the grape life cycle that produces good wine. Vintners have long known that unless a vine goes through a period of seeming death the grapes it produces will not be of premium quality. This is the reason that grapes grown in tropical climes, while they may be outwardly lush and beautiful, never seem to have the character of those grown in lands where Winter imposes a breathing spell that somehow results in better fruit.

The Napa Valley's climate is ideal for this process, since its daytime winter temperatures hover in the 50° range, and night time can go down below freezing. This is fine as long as the vines are dormant. The same temperatures during the Spring, when the sap has risen in the vines and the flowers have appeared, would be disastrous.

Winter is normally the season when the repairs and maintenance that are normal to winery care hit their peak. Fermentation tanks, especially those made of wood, must be scrubbed down, then sterilized with a burning sulphur candle. The resulting pungent sulphur dioxide gas is an active germicide, and thoroughly destroys all bacteria or wild yeasts that might otherwise result in a wine of dubious quality.

Another, more dramatic operation also takes place in the Winter. Right after an oaken aging tank is emptied of its contents, that tank must be rehabilitated. Sometimes, especially in a new tank, a thorough scrubbing down and sterilization will do, but in old cooperage, the tank may require a bit of drastic surgery. After many years of constant use, the wine has so thoroughly saturated a surface layer of oak that the tank no longer imparts its oaken characteristics but instead may carry over a flavor from a previous vintage;

Amidst a welter of hoses and steel fermentors, a cellarman at the Robert Mondavi Winery transfers wine from one tank to another in the complicated process that leads to superlative wine. *Right:* Near the Carmelite Monastery at the foot of the Oakville Grade, the pruned vines form a neat pattern leading to the eastern edge of the valley. This scene is in early February.

and that is not always desirable. In small fifty-five gallon cooperage this is solved by dismantling and cleaning the barrel, stave by stave, and then reassembling it. Larger oak casks, many of them holding thousands of gallons, are quite another matter. Building casks like this entails skilled labor, the best of materials, and generous amounts of money and some or all of these may be in short supply. The fine old casks of Inglenook, Beringer and Greystone are nearly a hundred years old, and are almost completely irreplaceable as aging tanks, let alone their value as art objects.

In cases of extreme deterioration, a thorough scraping of the inside surface of the tank so that a new layer of oak is exposed restores the tank's characteristics. This is a seldom used process, since the chances of ruining the tank are quite high, and is resorted to only when the cask is very valuable, or in such an advanced stage of deterioration that scraping is considered the last resort. Tanks are regularly scraped to remove the tartrates that accumulate during the aging process, and this, to a certain extent, helps reveal new wood and extend the useful life of a tank.

The fermentation of a new wine is an extremely active process, and one that produces numerous by-products as well as the primary wine. Many of these by-products remain suspended in the wine, and only a long rest will settle them out, unless some artificial means to achieve this end is employed. The old time vintner let nature do the settling, a process that usually took months, or years. His modern counterpart uses centrifuges or a settling process known as fining to clear the wine of suspended material, and produce the clean crystal clear wine that American tastes demands.

Fining may be done several times during the life of one vintage, or only once if the original treatment results in a suspension free wine. The usual material used is Bentonite, a type of infusorial earth that is mixed with water into a thin slurry then added to the tank's contents. The Bentonite settles to the bottom, taking with it the suspended material and leaving the wine clean and bright. Other materials such as gelatine solutions are sometimes used, but their purpose is always the same: to rid the wine of the suspended particles that do not particularly harm it, but certainly detract from its aesthetic appeal. There is considerable difference of opinion as to whether or not this detracts from the quality of a wine. Most vintners feel that it does not, while it immeasurably improves the appearance of a wine, and so enhances its acceptance by an increasingly critical public. Occasionally, a wine will "fall bright" without any outside help, and this is usually gleefully bottled and labeled as such, so there may be some virtue in abstention from the process.

Winter is a busy time in a winery, with much pumping, transferral of wines, and record keeping, but the single most important operation that takes place during the winter is the blending. This is, in effect, a marriage of wines.

Most wines, even the very finest, are blends. This does not mean that there is any adulteration involved in the negative sense, since the blending is usually undertaken to add some quality that even a very fine vintage may be lacking. The Cabernets of Bordeaux, for instance, by themselves are much too astringent, but the judicious addition of carefully calculated quantities of

Margot Venezia usually handles public relations for Oakville Vineyards, but during the annual First Crush celebration, she dons Bavarian costume and has a good time. *Right:* Inside one of Beaulieu Vineyard's huge stainless steel fermentors, a workman scrubs down the tank to a standard of cleanliness that would please the most meticulous housewife.

Merlot, a soft, comparatively bland wine, results in a product that is better than either one of its component parts, while still retaining the varietal characteristics of the Cabernet Sauvignon grape.

Blending, in a wine which will have a vintage year and a varietal label, is carefully controlled by law. A wine carrying a varietal name must be at least 51% of that grape, and have the distinctive characteristics attributed to it. If the wine is vintage dated, it must be 95% of that year. Places of origin given on a label are also subject to regulation. If the wine label says "Napa Valley" at least 75% of the total volume of that wine must have originated there. These are all minimum requirements, and happily, are usually exceeded by most premium producers. However since these requirements are law, they are strictly policed and enforced.

The vintner, before making a blend in quantity makes a carefully regulated batch that has the characteristics he desires. His guideposts are experience, a knowledgeable palate and the reaction of trusted tasters. If that blend falls within the limits imposed by the vintage bottling law, he will then mix his wine in quantity, age it and hope the whole process will result in a product he can market with pride as well as profit.

A winery with a large stock of its own wines has a distinct edge in the blending process. Not only are the characteristics of the wines thoroughly known, but since all of the components are made by one firm, they easily fall within the limits imposed by the label, which must state who made the major part of the bottle's contents. Smaller wineries must have a thorough knowledge of what their neighbor's or even competitor's tanks hold: a process which is approached with an enthusiasm that does much to enhance the Valley's reputation for outstanding hospitality.

Winter in the Napa Valley is relatively mild, but somewhat on the dampish side. Most of the 33 inches of rain that annually fall as an average in the Valley

In early March, the sun throws long shadows across the lawn of the Niebaum House, while in the valley the morning mists have yet to be dissipated by the sun. *Right:* In the Vineyard Room of Robert Mondavi's Winery at Oakville, well attended classical concerts enhance the winter social season.

comes during the Winter, to be sucked up by the soil and slowly trickled down to the roots, where it will feed the vines during the active growing periods of Spring and Summer.

Although some pruning is done in the Fall, immediately following harvest, most of it is done in Winter and early Spring before the vines actively began to grow. This is a most important process, since the skill with which it is done pretty much predicates the yield of that vineyard. The most vigorous spurs are selected, and pruned back so that only two, or at most three buds are retained on which flowers will sprout and eventually ripen as a bunch of grapes. Care must be taken to retain only enough buds so that the vine can supply enough nutrient to nourish the fruit it will bear, and keep a nice balance between quality and quantity. An incorrectly pruned vine will either produce too many grapes ("overcropping") which it will not be able to ripen, or well ripened grapes in small quantity. In the Napa Valley, where the emphasis is on quality, the latter practice is the lesser of two evils, but the optimum condition would be to have a vineyard pruned so that it produces the largest possible amount of correctly ripened grapes. For that reason, skilled pruners are very much in demand, since their judgment will directly influence the quality of next year's crop.

Most of the outdoor winter work in the Valley is sodden misery. The rain is cold, pervasive, while the fog streams in over the wooded crests of the mountains in tattered streamers, an army of fleeing ghosts. It is a season that must simply be endured if one is to taste the delights of Spring. In the snug homes, however, fireplaces are lighted, old port lovingly decanted, and preparation of meals becomes a high art. It is a season when old friendships are reaffirmed and new acquaintances become friends. New wines are tasted, new techniques are disclosed, and the ideas that will result in a better product next season are thoroughly discussed. The stage is being laid for the awakening.

The mists and rains of late Winter and early Spring may be a bit uncomfortable, but are necessary if the vines are to have the deep-down moisture which will nourish them during the hot days of Summer. *Right:* Pruning is usually done in the Winter, but it can be done immediately following the harvest in the mountains, where the vines become dormant very early. Here a worker trims off a cane, leaving only the strong spur which will bear new wood next year.

CHAPTER IX

THE AWAKENING — SPRING

Almost overnight, the air acquires a certain softness, a gentle haze cradles the increasing warmth, and in the vineyards the grey vines suddenly burst forth in a fringe of delicate green that presages the activity that is to come. The winter rains have already greened the tan hills, but now the flowers burst from the soil and paint the slopes with splashes of vivid color. Down in the Valley, the almond trees explode in puffy white clouds of blossoms, and the very air is somnolent with the drone of busy bees. Spring has come to the Napa Valley, and characteristically, it has come beautifully.

The Valley, which is outstanding any time of the year, is especially beautiful in March and April. It is a time of renascent life, of birth and beauty. The gaunt shapes of winter put on a lacework of tender green, the trees put out their shoots of new leaves, and gratefully lose the nakedness which they endured all winter.

Spring is a time of beauty, but it also is the most dangerous time of the whole year. Frost is an ever present danger, since new vines just emerging from the deep sleep of Winter can easily be killed by sub-freezing temperatures. New shoots are even more susceptible. Thirty minutes of sub-freezing temperatures can damage them to the extent that when the morning sun finally warms them, they wilt, blacken and die. There will be no crop this year from that particular vine.

It used to be that the only protection against this danger was to plant a vineyard on a hillside not susceptible to frost, or have an extremely good working relationship with, and faith, in the Almighty. Today, a few added safeguards are available, although few people would turn their backs on the old standbys.

One of the most common questions asked by visitors to the Valley is, "what is the function of the thirty-foot towers studding the vineyards?" These towers always mount an engine driving a large aircraft type windscrew, and are arranged in such a pattern that a breeze can be set up that covers all parts of the vineyards. They are such an intrinsic part of the landscape that most natives take them completely for granted, as though they had grown there.

These are wind towers, the first line of defense against frost. Sub-freezing air tends to be denser, and hence hugs the ground. If a breeze is set up the warmer upper air circulates over the vines and blossoms, and so helps to avert freezing. Until an awareness of air pollution made it impractical, smudge pots and orchard heaters were also used to supply that critical one degree that might spell the difference between freezing and survival. Smudging is frowned upon nowadays, but almost every orchard has a few heaters strategically located. One can always argue about the propriety of using this equipment, and the user can become extremely eloquent in its defense, especially if its use has saved his crop.

Most vineyardists rely on a most sophisticated method of frost fighting. The whole Valley is studded with water reservoirs which not only provide badly needed irrigation water during the critical growing periods up to about mid-June, but also serve as a standby frost protection system. A vineyard equipped with this sys-

A special tractor, designed specifically for vineyard use, takes much of the back-breaking work out of tending a vineyard, but the work still is hot and demanding. *Right:* The origin of the Zinfandel grape has been the subject of much speculation, but it has become the most classically "Californian" of all wine grapes. In the Napa Valley, it reaches a perfection that challenges even the lordly Cabernet.

tem will have a frost alarm which clangs lustily in the vineyardist's bedroom if the temperature should become critical. He may choose to fight the frost by turning on a sprinkler system that immediately warms his vineyard with a fine rain of above-freezing temperature water. If the temperature is cold enough to freeze the rain, he benefits by the fact that freezing water is an exothermic process which gives off heat. And lastly, the freezing process coats his tender young shoots with an insulating coat of ice, shielding them from the too-cold air. The young growth will not tolerate 31° for more than a half hour, but 32° seems to do no apparent harm. So a casing of ice, while apparently deadly, is in reality a gleaming lifesaver that can make the difference between a bearing vineyard and a zero crop.

The most highly visual sign of Spring in the Valley is the coat of bright yellow mustard weed that bursts into bloom between the rows of grey-brown grapevines. The origin of this floral display reads like something out of the Hansel and Gretel story. Legend has it that when Father Altimira first visited the Napa Valley in 1823, he carried with him a bag of mustard seed which intentionally had a small hole in it. This was mounted on one of his burros in such a manner that the motion of the animal allowed a thin trickle of seeds to drop. Retracing his steps a few months later must have been relatively simple: he simply followed the ribbon of growing gold that marked his previous trail.

However it got there, mustard is in the Valley's soil to stay, especially if the vineyardist has anything to say about it, and he most assuredly does. This cover crop not only prevents erosion but also adds a saffron slash of color to the Valley in the Spring, a not inconsiderable asset in a valley where beauty is part of everyday life. It is also a valuable cover crop which, turned into the soil in mid-Spring, provides a series of aquifiers and a valuable shot of green fertilizer.

Mustard weed is not only highly decorative in the springtime, but is also a valuable cover crop. *Right:* The helicopter is an invaluable tool for spraying a sulphur solution that keeps down mold in grapes almost right for the harvester's hand. In right background are the buildings of Sterling Vineyards.

Spring is also the time when the various diseases that can plague a vineyard are busily attacked. Helicopters and ground rigs are both used to spread the sulphur compounds that inhibit the oidium, commonly known as powdery mildew, that must be constantly fought lest it takes over a vineyard. In mountain plantings, a constant irritant is the poison oak that seems to flourish on even the poorest soil, and is always ready to add its irritating itch to the vineyardists list of troubles.

And that list is long! There are several dozen diseases that can attack a vineyard, and while only a few of them are common or widespread, they all require surveillance and constant vigilance. As soon as the rains have abated, the vineyardist is out on his land, scrutinizing every vine with an eye trained to spot the slightest abnormality, and ready to nip in the bud any disease that could affect his vineyard. Eternal vigilance is not only the price of freedom, but also of a healthy vineyard, and while to the casual observer a vineyardist may seem to be simply glorying in all the beauty that surrounds him on a sunny, balmy Spring day, he is really checking on all the problems that must be attended to now if he is to be happily busy in October.

Spring is a beautiful season in the Valley, but vineyardists understandably breath a sigh of relief when this gorgeous but potentially disastrous season has safely merged with Summer. Disaster can come any time of the year, but Spring is the time when it is most imminent, and the fact that it comes disguised in robes of transcendental beauty does not detract one iota from its potential deadliness.

Still, anyone falling under the magic spell of the new life, fragrant blossoms, and puffy, lazy white clouds hanging over a landscape whose beauty is daily refurbished and renewed will tell you that for all its potential danger, this is still the magic time of the year.

Spring brings rain, mist and flowering mustard. One of the many moods of the Napa Valley, it is one more aspect of a valley that is always changing. *Right:* Grape vines live almost a hundred years, and some exceptional specimens exceed even that. This sturdy specimen, one of the original Inglenook vines, is almost 80 years old and still producing vigorously, although most vines are replanted after about 40 productive years. *Pages 168-169:* Die-hard environmentalists may object to orchard heaters (they call them "stinkpots"), but a vineyardist who has had his crop saved by these heaters can become very vociferous in their defense. Ten of these diesel oil burning heaters and a wind machine, can raise the temperature of a vineyard 3 to 4 degrees per hour, and that can mean the difference between a crop or a crop failure.

CHAPTER X

THE LONG, HOT SUMMER

By the calendar, Summer arrives around the twenty-first of June, but to a vineyardist Summer starts once his vines have flowered and acquired the "set" that will grow into grapes. By mid May the vine has put forth buds which look very much like a miniature bunch of grapes, but before these can form into fruit, they must go through the flowering process. This usually happens in the first ten days of June, although hot weather can advance the date, or cold weather retard. The pale white flowers are so small, so seemingly insignificant that most visitors overlook them entirely, yet without them there would be no grapes in October; for this is the birth of a cluster, and unless conditions are just right: moderately dry, warm weather, the vines will not set a full crop of fruit, and the vineyardist will have a few acres of pretty green leaves to look at, but that's all.

If everything goes well, by late June the grape clusters are apparent and growing rapidly. Soon they will have attained the shape and number they will keep till harvest, and the vineyardist can begin to make some estimates of his crop. If it is unusually heavy, he may thin it to get optimum quality: a slow, arduous process which he does grudgingly while counting his blessings. In some varieties, he may partially defoliate his vines to allow sunshine into the interior so that clusters otherwise hidden by the leaves may ripen. It means long, hard, arduous hours in the vineyards, under conditions which can best be categorized as brutal. When the Bible mentions, as the epitome of hard labor, the work of the laborers in the vineyards, the vineyardist knows what it's all about. He's been there.

Still, the work must be done, and it must be done now if there is to be a crop later on. Summer in the Napa Valley, cooled as it is by its proximity to San Pablo Bay, is relatively mild, especially when compared to the infernoes of the inland valleys, but still counts several days where the mercury pushes past 100° F. This is the time when the heat units the vines need to ripen their fruit are accumulated. It is also the time for general maintenance in the fields. Suckers must be trimmed, canes tied and trained, and pesticides applied. There is no romance in tending a vineyard during the summertime, just hard work; and very often this is when a would-be vineyardist finds out if he has the stuff it takes to succeed in this game. During the long, hot summer the men get separated from the boys pretty quickly, and the blazing sun plays no favorites.

In July the tempo picks up a bit. As soon as the first blush of color appears on the grapes, equipment is readied. Tanks are washed down and sterilized, gondolas are painted and the mechanical devices with which all wineries abound are put through a "dry run" to make sure they are ready for the frenetic months ahead. Once that is done, there is little left to do except wait for the sun and mist to work their magic on the vines, now growing increasingly heavy with their loads of swelling fruit.

Summer is the big tourist season in the Valley, in spite of the fact that vines in Summer look like so many rows of dusty bushes. The twin roads that bracket the

By early Summer the grape clusters have formed and assumed the position they will hold till maturity. Careful vineyardists check the clusters for size, and if necessary, thin them, so that the remaining berries will achieve maximum quality. *Right:* It is near Summer's end and the grapes hang seemingly ripe on the vine, but the cool touch of fog off San Pablo Bay adds just the right touch of fruit acid that make Napa Valley wine so different, and so desirable.

Valley carry a never ending stream of cars that divert themselves into wineries' entrances until the parking lots are full, then keep on going till they hit the end of the Valley and turn back, hoping to find a hole in the unending stream of traffic. Residents of the Valley have known for years that Highway 29, on which most of the wineries front, is completely inadequate to carry the monstrous traffic loads imposed upon it. Nevertheless, if there is one single point on which the Valley stands united, it is in a fanatically firm opposition to a freeway, which they feel, would not solve their problem, but only aggravate it. The bureaucrats in Sacramento have finally gotten the message: In 1974 the last parcel of land acquired years ago for a freeway was returned to the purpose for which it is best suited: growing grapes. If the residents have anything to do with it, the freeways will never come to the Napa Valley.

The wineries long ago discovered that one of the very best ways to promote their product was to provide a few sips of it to whet the thirst of the potential customers. Thus, most wineries provide attractive tasting rooms to lure customers into loading a few cases of their product into the family car. By the large, they are extremely successful. Most wineries conduct tours of their premises the year round, with the possible exception of a few frantic days at the height of the crush, and usually end the tours in the tasting room. It is a very hardy soul, indeed, who can go the length of the Valley without having added a few bottles to his cellar or pounds to his waistline, or both.

Some wineries make this source of distribution their main sales effort, others use it only as an adjunct to a regular sales program. All find it highly lucrative, while the tourist finds it thoroughly enjoyable. No wonder the system flourishes!

Summer is also the season for festivals, of which there are quite a few in this valley where the enjoyment of life takes second place only to work. Charles Krug has for

The cellarmaster at Stony Hill reads the degrees Balling on his saccharometer, and is content. Another good vintage in the making. *Right:* The early morning sun backlights ripe Green Hungarian grapes in the Jerry Draper vineyards on Spring Mountain.

many years held festivals on its immaculately groomed lawns shaded by giant, several hundred years old oaks. Its August Moon concerts are of very high caliber employing the very best professional talent, and drawing audiences from the metropolitan centers. These concerts trend more toward the classics, and draw a sedate, pensive crowd. The grounds are also the scenes of a weekly wine tasting for selected customers and friends, where Peter Mondavi very proudly shows off the not inconsiderable talents of his winery.

Down the road, at his brother's winery, Robert Mondavi has a different kind of concert. Largely youth oriented, it features popular jazz bands and groups, which always draw capacity crowds, mostly through the front gates but also clandestinely through the vineyards. Again, wines are tasted, appreciated, discussed and bought. Everyone has a good time, except the harried caretakers who must pick up after a young crowd more dedicated to ecology in word than in fact.

Most of the wineries provide picnic tables or a pleasant place to open a bottle of wine from the obvious source to share with a lunch. The little park in the center of St. Helena does yeoman service, as does the public riverside park at Calistoga. Less well known are the Chinese pagodas at Chateau Montelena or the picnic tables at Burgess Cellars that have a view unequalled anywhere in the valley. A little off the beaten path, but well worth seeking out, is Crane Park, behind the High School in St. Helena. Well equipped with shade trees and picnic benches, it is a delightful spot, and well worth the effort it takes to find it.

Summer is a waiting time; a hush that comes over an audience just before the curtain raises for the main act. It is a time of preparation, of anticipation, and as the swelling grapes grow lush and full in the sun, all eyes are bent toward the drama that is soon to unfold.

The curtain rises . . .

The Moscato Cannelli grape is grown in only small quantities in the Napa Valley, but here, this luscious sweet grape attains a complexity that makes the wine produced from it always in short supply. This bunch is from the Charles Krug vineyard on the Oakville Grade. *Right:* Young shoots emerge from this mature vine, which has been pruned so that only its strongest spurs remain and bear fruit. Note the flower clusters, which will in time grow into grapes.

CHAPTER XI

THE CRUSH

The warm days of July and August have done their work, and on the vines the grapes hang, lush and ripe-looking, seemingly ready for the hand of the picker. All the hard work that has been done all year, all the hopes and expectations reach their culmination in late August or early September when the blush on the grape reaches its deepest hue, and the time of the crush is at hand.

Vineyardists who long to see their grapes safely off the vine and into the crusher point out that the fruit has reached the ultimate state of desirability, while more pragmatic winemasters, armed with refractometers opt for those few extra days that will give the grapes exactly the right balance of fruit acid and sugar that will result in a superlative wine.

Finally, the day comes when all these conditions are just right, and the pickers move into the vineyards. It is the opening gun in what can best be described as a military campaign.

On one side are marshalled all the negative forces that can impede the making of good wine. Their weapons are wind, rain, hail, too high temperatures and fog. Their allies are flocks of voracious birds who can each easily eat their own weight in grapes each day, and deer that can jump an eight-foot fence, or wriggle through a hole that would present a challenge to a small boy. These graceful, beautiful and extremely destructive scavengers will eat anything the birds have missed, down to the wood of the main vine itself. Bees may not seem like much of a problem, but their voracious appetite for the juicy nectar of the grape accounts for many tons that would otherwise become wine. Also allied against the vintner are cantankerous machines that can break down at the most inopportune time, and the ever present human errors that can negate even the best efforts. But the biggest enemy of all, and the most implacable, is time.

It takes a beautiful synchronization of events to turn a grape into wine, and every one of them is based on good timing. There is an optimum time for a grape to be picked; it must reach the crusher within a few hours, it must be crushed at the right sugar level, and the fermentation must take place within carefully definite limits of temperature. Any number of things can go wrong that will turn that beautiful load of grapes into so much spoiled must good for nothing except to fertilize a vineyard.

On the other hand, the vintner has quite a few things going in his favor—otherwise wine would be even more scarce and expensive than it is. For one thing, a ripe grape is a natural wine factory that only needs its skin to be broken to spontaneously begin operations. Vintners will tell you that they do not themselves make wine: wine makes itself. All they do is direct it a bit, here and there. Their job is to assist nature wherever their intervention will help or speed things up. Then, too, the making of wine is not the haphazard affair it was way back, when, for the first time some caveman inadvertently squashed some grapes and so started the whole wine industry. Over the centuries, a store of knowledge has accumulated that can predicate with a certain amount of reliability what will happen once the

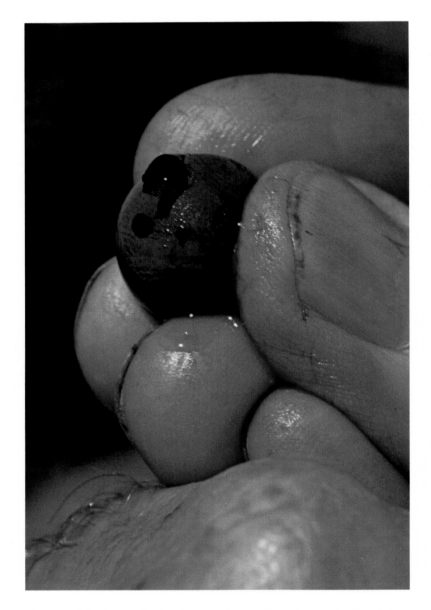

Vineyardists know that when a star pattern forms in the juice squeezed from a grape, the fruit is close to optimum ripeness, and ready for the crush. *Right:* Balancing a 40 pound load isn't easy, but this young man, hurrying through the golden glory of a backlighted vineyard with his lug of Cabernet Sauvignon grapes, makes it look like play.

grapes have been consigned to the crusher. It's a good thing the vintner has a few things going for his side, because the obstacles are certainly many, and formidable.

While the rule of thumb is that grapes will be ready for picking 50 days after the first color appears, this is at best a rough approximation, especially in white grapes. Some harvests can begin as early as the last week in August, especially if the weather has been hot and dry, or linger on into November if rain and cold weather have been prevalent. Also, different vintners would pick the same vineyard at different times, depending on their requirements. Jack Davies will pick his Pinot Noir grapes at 19° Balling to make his superlative champagne, because he values fruit acid and low sugar. Robert Mondavi would prefer a 23.5° Balling for his Pinot Noir varietals. The usual difference is time, which allows the sugar to build up to the Mondavi requirements, while an early picking would suit Jack Davies' requirements better.

It is a very fortunate circumstance that different species of grapes ripen at different times, else the wineries would experience a few days of phenomenal glut. Even as it is, it takes a master tactician to juggle the time schedules so that the right grapes arrive at the proper time. If one grower goes off schedule it throws off all the rest: a situation which, if often repeated, is not particularly guaranteed to enhance the guilty one's popularity with his peers. As a general rule, white grapes ripen first, while the last Cabernet Sauvignons are often picked during the first rains of November.

While new techniques of grape picking have been introduced, the time honored method of picking the crop cluster by cluster still predominates. By the dawn's early light, the pickers move into the fields well bundled up against the pervasive chill of the fog, and further ward off the cold by setting a terrific pace during the cool morning hours. Later, when the sun has dissipated the mist, and the heat of the day has set in, there will be time to slow down, to pace oneself so that there is still enough steam left by quitting time to enjoy a can of beer and some good natured banter with his friends.

The crush is the time of year toward which all other efforts have been pointed. All the preparation, all the planting, cultivating, pruning and trimming have been aimed toward this time, when the fruit leaves the vine and trades one life for another. Wine is unique in that it is a living entity, with a cycle of birth, youth, maturity and death and the cycle starts here, during crush.

Like most birth cycles, the crush is dramatic and sometimes a bit messy. After the grapes have been cut from the vines and piled into the brightly colored lug boxes, they are dumped into a gondola, which, after being weighed, is tilted by a hoist so that its contents are dumped into the crusher. A helical worm (screw) pushes, shoves and moves the fruit into the crusher, while the motion of the stemmer separates the leaves and stems from the new must. In red wines the must is pumped, in a pulpy, liquid state, to its tank where it will ferment for from four to six days. The pulped fruit will float on top of the solution, forming a cap, over which the new wine is pumped twice a day. The alcohol that is a product of fermentation dissolves the pigmentation in the skins, and gives the wine its characteristic color. Roses are allowed to stay on the skins only long enough to pick up a little color, while whites have

Joe Heitz inoculates a batch of new wine with a strain of yeast which will produce the characteristics he likes in his wine. The yeast comes from the Institut Pasteur, in Paris, France, and is carefully cultured, year after year, to produce the same predictable results. *Right:* The hands of a grape cutter, skilled, strong and knowing, support a cluster of Zinfandel grapes before the swift stroke that will separate it from the vine and send it on its way to a new life, as wine.

practically no contact with the pulp. In making white wine, the free run juice is piped directly to a fermentation tank, while the pulp is pressed immediately to get out all the rest of the juice. This is added to the free run, and contributes some tannic qualities to the wine that aids it in the aging process. The juice is fermented out of contact with the pulp.

While grapes are being crushed, a measured amount of potassium metabisulphite is thrown into the must to kill any bacteria and wild yeasts that may be on the grapes. The resulting solution is then impregnated with a strain of yeast whose characteristics are well known, and the fermentation starts.

A tank of red wine in full fermentation is really a sight to behold for the fermentation of sugar produces approximately equal parts (by weight) of alcohol and carbon dioxide. The carbon dioxide is released as bubbles which induce a great, rolling boil in the tank, as though some submerged monster were in its death throes. The fermentation process also releases heat, and this must be dissipated, else the whole batch could be spoiled. This is one reason that fermentation tanks in Europe were almost always in cool cellars and caves; the cool temperatures helped to keep the wine tank and its contents within acceptable temperature limits. Nowadays, the heat of fermentation is controlled by jacketed tanks through which refrigerant is piped, so that the modern vintner has complete control of his fermentation every step of the way. In making white wine, the degree of activity is controlled by keeping the juice just barely above that temperature point where fermentation is possible. This process, known as cold fermentation, is now common practice in the Valley and has done much to develop the outstanding character and fruitiness of Napa Valley wines.

It is certainly a far cry from the system of only a few years ago when the method used was basically to crush the grapes, dump them in a tank, and pray. Modern vintners become quite religious during the crush, but they also have a few means of control in their own right. It is true that a grape has everything within itself that is needed to make wine, and it is itching to do just that, but somehow the process always seems to work much better if a little intelligent help is administered wherever it will do the most good. The secrets of the grape are being systematically unravelled, so that every year we come closer and closer to the time when all the secrets will be known, and so capable of being controlled. Still, as one knowledgeable winemaker puts it:

"We've come a long way in the last few years, but we still have a long way to go ere we get out of the grape everything that God created . . . but we're working at it!"

There is a special atmosphere in the Valley during the crush, an air of excitement that pervades everything. From the first pre-dawn rumble of the gondolas on their way to the fields, through the rush of the day, to the cool nights where lights glare above the still busy crushers, there is something that would let even the most blase stranger know that this is a special time. After the first week, the odor of newly fermented wine hangs like a perfume over the whole Valley adding not a little to the feeling of excitement and bustle that are characteristic of this time. This is the time of the last battle in the campaign, and it is one that must be won if there is to be a prize.

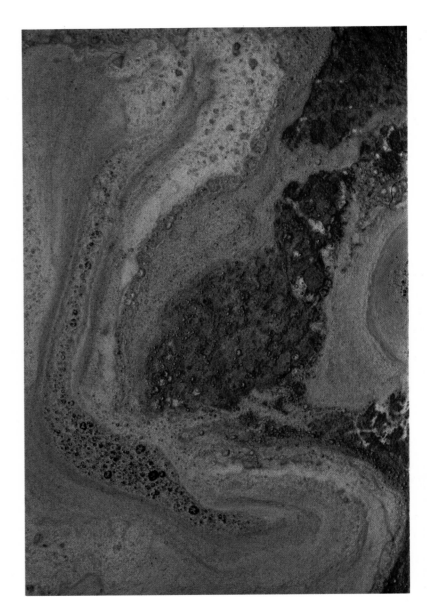

New red wine, pumped into a sump forms a pattern of swirls and bubbles. This new wine still contains much of the carbon dioxide which is a by-product of fermentation. *Right:* At Louis Martini Winery, red wine is drawn from the bottom of the concrete fermentor vat and pumped over the cap. The alcohol in the new wine dissolves pigment in the skins and so gives the wine its distinctive ruby tint.

During this period the whole energies of the Valley are dedicated toward the ending of the grape-growing cycle. There are few parties during this time of the year; everyone is too busy, and too tired. The parties will come . . . and with a vengeance, once the harvest is safely in the barn, the new wines are sleeping in their tanks, and the weary vintner can afford to rest from his labors. It's really what he's been working for all year, and yet when crush is done, he heaves a sigh of relief and nevertheless feels vaguely discontented. The battle is over, and he has won, but he somehow misses the fighting. That feeling won't last too long: he has other battles to fight before his infant wines grow up and release their joy to a waiting world.

The vineyardist whose grapes are picked early is the one who can relax. Not so the man with a hundred acres of grapes whose sugar is not quite right, or who has varieties currently not much in demand. Every year some grapes may be bypassed, and hang on the vines because there is no demand for them. It's one of the breaks of the game, and a bitter one. Fortunately, the new plantings in the Valley, now just coming into production, are all of highly sought after varieties of which there is usually a shortage. Little by little older vineyards planted to Burger or Golden Chasselas—species much in demand years ago but now no longer in vogue —are being replaced by Cabernet Sauvignon, Pinot Noir, and Pinot Chardonnay, for which the demand seems endless, as long as there are tanks available to store the wine.

The crush reaches its peak by the middle of September, and continues full blast for almost a month. By the middle of October there are signs of slackening, although there is still plenty of activity in the later-maturing red wines. By the end of October, the end is in sight, and the weary vintner begins cleaning up the mess he didn't have time to take care of during the harried days when he was crushing grapes.

Finally, it's all over. The new wines are gently bubbling in their tanks, or safely sleeping in their oaken casks, and another vintage, the latest in a long line going back thousands of years, has been completed. Now is the time to call a few friends, set a festive board, and taste the new wines. It will take months to properly evaluate them, for they are still children, and need much growing up. Still, a man can always call upon his friends for a pleasant task such as this one, secure in the knowledge that tomorrow it will be his neighbor's tank he is sampling and evaluating.

Many a man, in the twilight of his life, will tell you that the best years he ever spent were his years in military service. Forgotten are all the bad, even hideous things, while the comaraderie, the pranks and the good times become even better in the retelling when they have achieved the patina of age. So it is with the crush. It's work, hard work, yet each year the vintner looks forward to it, perhaps with a sigh of resignation and a few complaints, yet secretly revelling in the fact that he is a man doing a man's work, and glorying in it. It was ever thus. It may very well forever so be.

Part of the continuous research that this winery sponsors, these experimental wines at Robert Mondavi, in five gallon lots, will be carefully evaluated for a possible outstanding lot. This area, under the supervision of a graduate enologist, is known in the plant as "Chateau Jones". *Right:* New wine, just a few days old, is being drawn from the bottom of the fermenting tank and run into this filtered sump. From here, it will be pumped over the cap, in the process leaching out more color from the pigment in the skins, which is soluble in alcohol. *Pages 184-185:* This happily intoxicated bee is too drunk to walk, let alone fly. Feeding on the fermented nectar that exudes from the grapes it punctures with its sharp proboscis (note grape directly in front of bee), these insects account for thousands of tons of wasted grapes that would otherwise become wine.

CHAPTER XII

LA DOLCE VITA

As any student of human affairs well knows, the lives and characters of a people are definitely influenced by the environment in which they live. The fabled islands of Polynesia produce a cheerful, happy people: a reflection of the earthly paradise in which they live, while the craggy islands of the North Atlantic rear a people strong in mind and body, but not particularly noted for gaiety or laughter. It might even be said that a person is a child of the environment in which he has his being, for the forces at work on his personality are so strong that he is either consciously or subconsciously molded in a pattern that fits the land in which he lives.

Any place that produces the good things of life liberally and has a strong personality of its own is bound to produce its own life-style which will be a reflection of the environment in which it exists. So it is in the Napa Valley, which has evolved a way of life which is distinctly its own, and which is the envy of anyone who has ever sampled it. Given the beauty of this valley, it is no wonder that it exerts a charm so strong that every year it claims thousands of willing victims.

Wine lands are traditionally happy lands, where laughter and song are as much a part of the fabric of life as hard work. When there is work to be done, let it be done willingly, but laughter speeds the weary hours and helps lighten what would otherwise be an intolerable load. And when the crush is done and the new wines are slumbering in their oaken cradles, then there is time for fun and relaxation, for gaiety and song to celebrate a task well done. The early wine festivals were always tied to the end of the harvest period, and if they sometimes got a bit exuberant, it was only because the celebrants entered into the spirit of things, and like a new wine, sometimes got out of hand.

The Napa Valley is no exception to this general rule. In fact, it has developed a few traditions of its own, some of which have been handed down from the various sources of the Valley's culture, and others which have evolved from local conditions. Like all wine lands, it is a place where the local social customs are tied to the phases of the wine year, from the comparative quiet of Summer to the frenetic activity of the crush.

Climate is always a major factor in determining the social customs of a region and here the Valley is singularly blessed. Shielded by its mountains and inland location, yet adjacent to a major body of water, the climate is generally Mediterranean, with a rainy yet mild Winter and Spring; a warm, sometimes hot Summer, and an Autumn that can drag seductive, summer-like days into early November. It is a climate made to order for out of doors living and entertainment and the Valley indulges it to the full. Outdoor entertaining is the order of the day and most social functions during all but the three rainiest months take place out of doors. The tremendous success of the Charles Krug August Moon programs and the Robert Mondavi Summer Series can be traced not only to the general excellence of the programs, but also to the beautiful surroundings in which they are held. There is something about relaxing on a well kept lawn, in the shadow of the encircling mountains, and having one's senses lulled into a soothing

A comely young resident of the Napa Valley, relaxed beside Tom Lynch's pool on the Silverado Trail; and adds a definitely decorative touch to the scenery. *Right:* In her private hilltop pool, near Oakville, Mary Anne Gamble enjoys the sweet life of the Napa Valley.

euphoria by good wine, good food, and good music that is extremely pleasant: an attainment of that good life which is the seldom achieved goal of people all over the world. The Napa Wine Library tastings probably would be successful under any circumstances, but certainly, are enhanced by being held under the giant oaks of the Niebaum Mansion in the surroundings that once enthralled the legendary Captain, and which still weaves their spell of enchantment to this day.

While the gentle climate and easygoing attitude of the Valley seemingly foster a casual state of life and attire it is also a place that brings out the best in everyone, and the natural sense of beauty that the Valley so freely evokes is evidenced, especially in the upper social levels, in beautiful accoutrements, clothes and manners. The style of living, by long association, seems perfectly natural to the inhabitants of the Valley, but is of a superlatively high order to others accustomed to a different, less favored level. Small wonder it is that the Napa Valley life-style, has become the envy of those forced by fate to exist in other, less favored locales.

This way of life has the force of tradition, for from its very earliest days the Valley enjoyed an eclectic culture derived from the people who had elected to make this place their home, The Krugs, Schrams, de Latours, Carpys, Beringers, Parrots were all well educated, cultured people, with a natural sense of beauty and decorum. They early established codes of conduct and behavior that became the rules for the Valley: and those rules, set in a gentler, more formal era, have achieved the status of tradition over the years, and are largely followed even to this day. They may be a little old fashioned, like the streetlights of St. Helena, but if so, they are delightfully old fashioned, and usually very much appreciated even by young people who have not been over-exposed to this type of living. The fact that these are the people who have the most enthusiasm for the Valley and its way of life would seem to indicate that the values exemplified here are basic, and desirable to people of all ages and social strata.

The high degree of sophistication that is so evident in the Valley can partly be traced to this tradition of eclecticism, but also to the fact that living costs in the Valley are so high that newcomers to it have usually had most of the cultural advantages that affluence customarily fosters. Many of the new vintners in the Valley are people who have attained considerable success in other fields of endeavor, but who have found in the wine scene a more desirable way of life, and in the Napa Valley a place where that way of life can be implemented. Thus, Fred McCrea came from the field of advertising, Jack Davies from business management, Mike Stone from the paper business, Donn Chappellet from automated food vending, and Joe Phelps from construction. These men brought not only the drive and expertise in business that had made them successes in their own fields, but also sophisticated living tastes that found a natural expression in the Valley. Others not directly connected with the wine scene also make the Valley their home. Arthur Hailey, when he isn't completely engrossed in writing his highly successful novels, splits his time between his home in the Bahamas and the Valley, George Gamble manages his huge cattle ranches from his hilltop home in Oakville, and Bill Stafford, who writes musical comedies for Las Vegas and

If this bottle could only talk! Part of the Joe Heitz collection, which he acquired from the Crocker estate, it bears the date 1816 (the year after Waterloo!!) and was lovingly decanted at a dinner for ten convivial souls, along with a 1934 Chateau La Tour, a 1929 Montrachet, a 1945 Beaulieu Cabernet Reserve, a 1964 Chateau La Tour, a 1945 Mouton-Rothschild, and a hundred year old brandy that was a warm silken sunshine. Really an evening to remember . . . and part of the good life in the Napa Valley. *Right:* The aging room of Heitz Cellars not only holds priceless wines, but is also the scene of some very well appreciated dinners. Hospitality is legendary in the Napa Valley and no one outdoes Joe and Alice Heitz.

Hollywood happily hangs his hat in his home over-looking the Silverado Trail. The Valley abounds in talent of all kinds, often completely unrelated to the wine industry, but united in a common love for a place where life can be lived to the full, and in the company of people who are pleasant, productive, and compatible.

In a region that is largely rural and some distance from the amenities of a large urban center, it is only natural that hospitality in the home would take the place usually filled by nightclubs and fancy restaurants. And the hospitality of the Napa Valley is legendary! In a place where seemingly every hostess has graduated from cooking school, or could have written the book, good cooking is taken for granted, and superlative cookery is common. The traditional fare of the world's wine countries has been supplemented here by the contributions of local cooks, some of whom have more than a touch of genius. When Simone Beck, the nationally renowned French Grande Dame of the gourmet world put on a cooking school for a selected few students who wanted instructions in the very best, and were willing to put up $1,500 each to attend her course, it was only natural that she should hold her school in the Napa Valley. She drew passing marks from the Valley cooks who audited her course, but not the awe which was accorded her elsewhere.

As one who has feasted at the best tables in the Valley, I can testify that wine country cuisine is bountiful, inventive, and so tasty that a prolonged stay in the Valley poses a threat to the waistline that is overcome only with many hard sets of tennis. Good food goes naturally with good wine, and in the Italian style, are inseparable. Since the life-style in the Valley is largely Italianate, it goes without saying that wine is part of every meal except breakfast, and does much to foster the reputation of the Valley as a gastronomical paradise.

A flight over the Valley shows that swimming pools and tennis courts are an essential part of its way of life. Pools are in use nine months of the year, and tennis is a year round sport. There are several well patronized golf courses in the Valley, and one of them, the Silverado, is host to the Kaiser Invitational which brings the world's finest golfers to this part of the country. Horseback riding is a natural sport in these beautiful rolling hills, and on any pleasant day the backroads are dotted with bike riders and backpackers who are enjoying a leisurely and closeup inspection of this, one of Nature's loveliest places. Life is good in the Valley, and those who love it for the many facets of its attraction live the good life on a daily basis, and take it as a normal part of living in this delightful spot.

Life in the Valley is mostly rural, but that doesn't mean that it is deficient in cultural activities. St. Helena boasts the Silverado Museum, one of the finest small museums in the country. This is the gift of Norman Strouse, a retired advertising executive who saw a chance to share with an appreciative public his collection of Robert Louis Stevenson memorabilia. Vintage Hall is a delightful museum dedicated to the practice of viticulture in the Valley from the earliest days to the present, and an attraction that daily draws more and more people. The Napa Valley Symphony and Napa Community College are cultural assets of the first water, and the delightful nearby city of Napa has all the amenities of a small metropolis. For those who crave

A visitor to the Napa Valley is introduced to a very civilized Napa Valley custom by Margaret Biever, center, and Johnsye Dietz. After three hard sets of tennis, champagne served in silver goblets cools the fevered brow and makes a pleasant game even better. *Right:* A page out of America's yesterday, a Sunday band concert in Lyman Park in St. Helena is enjoyed by people from the whole Valley.

something more grandiose San Francisco is only an hour away.

Some people live in the Valley and make their living in "The City," as San Francisco is universally designated. While the price and availability of gasoline may have some small effect on this arrangement, it will hardly destroy it. The people who can afford to commute to jobs in The City feel they have the best of two worlds, and they are not about to give up that delightful situation. High priced gasoline and rising at five a.m. are small prices to pay for the privilege of living in the Valley, especially when dawn breaking over the eastern mountain rim is such an entrancing spectacle.

God was indeed smiling the day He created the Napa Valley. Even if it did not produce some of the world's finest wines, it would still be a delightful spot in which to live; but enhanced as it is by Nature's gifts and the contributions of gifted men and women, it becomes the mecca of multitudes who feel that since they have but one life to live, they will live it in the most enchanting spot available. Unfortunately, it is not available to everyone, but still it can shine as a sought after dream, a place of vicarious enjoyment that forever keeps alive the flame of hope and ambition

As the poet Robert Browning put it: "Man's reach should exceed his grasp, or what's a Heaven for?"

The Napa Wine Library Tasting is a summer social event in which the whole Valley takes part. Good wines are appreciatively tasted, and who could say "no" to a comely young server such as this one? *Right:* Part of Polly Solari's extensive collection of wine glasses from around the world. These glasses show the tastes of former centuries, when wine was not as clear as it is today and glasses were not only receptacles, but also, in their own right, art objects.

CHAPTER XIII

OF VINES AND MEN

Critics of American wines have a few favorite subjects that they belabor unceasingly. While some of these criticisms are merely personal judgments that are expounded at length because a large part of the pleasure attendant to wine drinking comes from talking about it, others have a solid basis in fact and are worthy of discussion on their own merit. Of these, one of the most often discussed is the matter of names for wine.

Back in the early days of the wine industry, when the clientele was not nearly so sophisticated, names didn't matter much. Wine was bought by the barrel, was either white or red, and as long as it was potable, was accepted at face value without too much worry as to its pedigree. As quantity and quality increased and wine became a major item of commerce, individual vintners sought to identify their product by a recognizable name, and so the need arose to identify the wine more fully.

Count Agoston Haraszthy inadvertently solved one problem, and created another, when he brought back from Europe thousands of grape cuttings that were to provide the vines for the California wine industry. With a few notable exceptions, these cuttings were identified by species, and place of origin. This provided an easy, if not wholly accurate way to identify the wines that were soon to be made from the grapes sprouting from those cuttings.

A number of facts soon became apparent from the Haraszthy project, and one of the most startling was that wine made from grapes grown in California could be, and usually was, far different than that made from that same specie in its native land. A Cabernet grown in California had a fullness and softness quite unlike that grown in Bordeaux, a fact that often made 100% varietal wines a possibility. Vintners have long known that climate and soil induce changes in the vine, and the fruit it bears, and here, in this new land with its rich undepleted soil, a completely different kind of grape was being grown. It is true that the main characteristics of the parent vine were retained, but the differences were great enough to be discernible even to the untrained palate.

Purists argued that any change from the classic grapes of Europe were deficiencies, but more pragmatic persons who had tasted the new wines were quick to note that the differences were not necessarily bad, and in some cases were very definite improvements.

It must be remembered that the wine industry in California was still in its infancy and tied by tradition to the established wine countries of Europe. Also the newly affluent American public tended to look down on anything produced in America, especially wine, as definitely inferior. Since these constituted a good part of the new industry's potential clientele, their wishes of necessity were considered. And so a golden opportunity was bypassed, and the magnificent new wines of the Napa Valley were marketed under names like "California Burgundy" or "Chablis," which they definitely were not.

Immediately after Prohibition the opportunity to give meaningful names to the wines produced in the Valley was once more presented, and again rejected in

A man in his element, Peter Mondavi is at home in his vineyard, with a glass of his own good wine in his hand. *Right:* It is Summer's end and this cluster of Pinot Noir grapes, dusty, and slightly sunburnt, is ready for picking.

the name of expediency. And so, to this day, we have a generic name like "Burgundy" covering anything made with red grapes, and "Chablis" practically any white wine.

In spite of the fact that the wine snob has a tendency to look down on the generic wines, they are usually good, honest wines, and often very fine value. I know of one "Burgundy" which I am going to buy in quantity in 1976 for I was there when a load of prime Cabernet Sauvignon grapes unexpectedly filled the Cabernet tank to capacity before half the load was crushed. The balance, for lack of fermenting space, went into the "Burgundy" tank, much to the vintner's chagrin. He had to pay Cabernet prices for a wine which will be largely from a noble grape, but which he must sell at a much lower price. His loss is the customer's gain, for that wine in spite of its humble name will have most of the characteristics of the much higher priced Cabernet Sauvignon.

With the growing importance and reputation of Napa Valley attention is once more being given to the idea of naming wines produced in the Valley with names that have some local connection. "Rutherford" may not sound as elegant as "Chateau Latour" but the wine produced there can be equally good and the public would soon learn the names they equate with quality. Also under consideration is the idea of a distinctively shaped bottle that would say "Napa" as eloquently as the bottles of Bordeaux or Burgundy identify their own regions. There are some good brains working on this idea, and their possessors are not in the habit of wasting their time.

There has been much talk, especially by wine writers who haven't been to the Valley lately of the overproduction of wine grapes that should peak out in 1977. This is assuming that no new production facilities are installed in the Valley before that time, and that the newly planted vineyards bear their usual crop. It is a distinct possibility, of course, but one that has been anticipated. There is much new production expansion slated for the next few years, and since the market for the best Napa Valley wines seems to be practically unlimited, the Valley can ride out this crisis not only with a minimum of dislocation, but even with its usual profit. The new plantings are all of the most sought after varieties, and their grapes should find a home in the Valley, although the inflated prices of 1972 and 1973 probably will not be paid again. Those were the vineyardists' golden years, but are reflected in the high prices of wine now reaching the market.

The new emphasis in the Napa Valley is toward varietal wines; partly because they can command a better price, but also because these wines best exploit the characteristics of the Valley's soil and climate. The Valley seemingly can grow anything in the vinifera family, and very well. In 1973 it even proved that a hitherto unattained goal was possible.

Freemark Abbey is very fortunate that three of its general partners own extensive and excellent vineyards in the Valley. Naturally, these men see to it that their best grapes find a home in their own winery. In September, 1973, there were two days of drizzly rain, followed by warm and humid weather, conditions much desired in the Sauternes region of France, because it fosters the growth of *botrytis cinerea*, the "noble rot" that produces

A large part of the good life in the Napa Valley can be understood by looking at this picture of Jamie Davies, a busy, active mother, who still has time to love, and be loved, by her children. *Right:* Fall brings a blaze of glory to the Valley, here exemplified by Napa Gamay leaves in their last flush of color.

the sweet and luscious wines for which the region is famous. Lawrie Wood noticed that a large section of his Conn Creek vineyard was infested with a mold that had all the classic appearances of botrytis. Tests proved that it was indeed the much sought after "noble rot," and thirty six tons of grapes were affected with it.

Botrytis penetrates the skin of a grape and draws off the moisture, thus increasing the sugar content. Those White Riesling grapes, at harvest had a sugar content of 30° B and produced a heavy, sweet wine very much like the wines of Sauternes and quite unlike the usual Johannisberg Riesling it normally would have made. The wine is a classic, and worth whatever price the vintner puts on it, because those conditions that produced it are a "once in a lifetime" proposition that may never again be repeated, much as it would be desired.

The slogan "cities are what people make them" is well known, and can be applied as well to the Napa Valley, for not only does the Valley mold the character of the people who make this their home, but it has itself been shaped by the men and women who have lived in this place. Charles Krug, Gustave Niebaum, the Beringer brothers, Charles Carpy, George de La Tour, Jacob Schram and more lately John Daniel and Louis Martini, all have left their mark on this valley, and have influenced the lives of the men who today carry on the work that they started.

The pioneer winemakers would be proud of the new breed that carry on the tradition of excellence that they founded. Andre Tchelistcheff, the legendary winemaker of Beaulieu Vineyards is retired now, but is still active as a consultant, and the men he trained are leaders in the industry. One doesn't become a leader in this industry without having some very positive ideas about wine, and it is not at all unusual to find diametrically opposite views on the same subject emanating from people who each have a cadre of devoted followers. The wonderful thing about this situation is that these people can differ strongly on some facet of winemaking, yet be close personal friends and mutual admirers. There are, however, a few people who seemingly rise above all others, and are held in high esteem by all. Two of these certainly would be Brother Timothy of the Christian Brothers, and Hanns Kornell.

Brother Timothy's long period of service in the Napa Valley alone would entitle him to respect, but it is the man's basic kindness that most endears him to his friends. A shrewd bargainer and a hard competitor, he nevertheless would be the first to extend a helping hand to anyone needing it, and this is the fact that most endears him to his peers.

Hanns Kornell is a unique combination of generosity, honesty, and integrity blended with a generous dosage of talent. An immigrant from Germany, he has become such an integral part of the Valley that it seems he must have been born here. There is no other Hanns Kornell in Germany or for that matter anywhere else in the world, but if there were, the air fare to the Napa Valley could easily be raised by popular subscription, such is the popularity of the genial German from Mainz.

A list of the interesting or productive people in the Valley would simply be a roster of the vintners doing business there. It is a place that fosters quality, and the track is so fast that only the best survive. Men like Joe

Hans Kornell, certainly one of the most popular and respected citizens in the Napa Valley, likes to recall that back in 1940, as a practically penniless refugee from Nazi Germany, he spent a night in the Calistoga jail because he wasn't carrying the proper papers. A plaque saying "Hanns Kornell slept here" wouldn't seem out of place now. *Right:* An elegant setting for an aristocrat of wine. The 1973 Freemark Abbey Edelwein is a once in a lifetime experience that demands, and gets, the very finest care. *Pages 200-201:* Spring is in the Valley and the almond trees etch a pattern of lacy white blossoms against a blue sky. This scene is near the Carmelite Monastery, looking towards the eastern mountains.

Heitz, Jim Nichelini, Bob and Peter Mondavi, Louis Martini, Bud Van Loben Sels, Jack Davies, Brother Timothy, Fred McCrea and Donn Chappellet to name only a few of the many who should be, can't help but make a place electric with their own personal magnetism, and even a few minutes spent with these men shows why they have achieved success and risen to the top of their profession. It takes talent, hard work, and drive to be a vintner anywhere, but in the Napa Valley, where the race is held between the admitted leaders in the field, these qualities are the bare minimum. It's that little extra touch of genius that makes the difference, and when that quality was being handed around, the Valley's vintner went around for a second helping.

What does the future hold for the Valley? That, of course, is unknown, although some reasonably safe predictions based on available data can be made.

As America becomes more conscious of things vinous and appreciative of the wines produced here, the Napa Valley can expect to increase its already dominant share of the market for fine table wines. More and more people are discovering that fine wine is one of the more worthwhile pleasures in life, and are taking part in that experience by laying down stores of choice vintages in their own cellars, so that wines acquired in their youth can mature into the nobility which is their natural heritage. While a Napa Valley Cabernet may be completely drinkable at four years of age, it will improve immeasurably if it is laid away to bottle age and achieve the silky smoothness and character that only time can give. Drinking such a wine when it is young is an act of infanticide, but it inevitably will be done until Americans learn that the fruits of patience can be very rewarding, and act accordingly. Fortunately, the trend is growing. Good cellars are proliferating, and in them, the noble wines of the Napa Valley sleep, patiently waiting for the time when their bounty will be released, and add a touch of beauty to the life of man.

As for the Valley itself, it will almost certainly continue to be a rural area, unless complete madness engulfs the powers that decide these things. It will certainly continue its dedication to quality, because that fits with the Valley's character and has proven that it is the right path to take. As America becomes more sophisticated in things vinous, the Valley certainly will be more appreciated and come into its own. The people there hopefully will retain the way of life they have evolved, and guard it zealously so that their children may some day enjoy an enclave of beauty in an increasingly ugly world.

It is that beauty that haunts people who have been exposed to it, for the need of beauty is as deep and basic, as deeply rooted in the soul of a sensitive person as is the need for food and drink. It is no wonder that my mind often wanders back to the Valley, to see again the delicate tracery of light and shadow on the face of Mt. St. Helena, to roam once more those verdant hills, blue with the lupine of spring, tawny with the gold of summer. I see the vineyards blossom yellow with mustard, grow green with summer, and wear once more their autumnal robes of purple and gold. I see the fruit hang on the vine, swollen with nectar, inviting one to taste its sweetness, and I know that once more, in spirit, I am in my beloved Napa Valley . . .

I lift my glass to you.

White blossoms against an azure sky, the humming of bees, the caress of a gentle breeze . . . Spring in the Napa Valley. *Right:* It is quite easy to tell red wine grapes from white once the colors of Autumn have painted the vines. Red grape leaves turn red; white grape leaves turn gold, as in this picture looking toward the eastern mountain rim near Stag's Leap.

GLOSSARY

AGING:
The process wherein wine is stored in oaken barrels or cask so that complex changes that only time can implement take place in the wine. Aging smooths a rough, new wine, adds bouquet and character. Most aging takes place in the oaken or redwood tank, although some changes also take place in the bottle.

ALLUVIAL FANS:
Soil deposits brought down from the mountains by streams and deposited in the valley.

AROMA:
The particular odor of a specific grape. Not to be confused with bouquet, although a wine has both.

BASKET PRESS:
A type of press wherein grapes are put in a wooden tub with slotted sides. Pressure applied by means of a large screw crushes the grapes and allows the juice to run out through the slots.

BIG WINE:
A wine of powerful and distinctive characteristics.

BOTRYTIS CINEREA:
A fungus which dries up the moisture in a grape and raises sugar content. Very desirable, in spite of its unprepossessing appearance.

BOUQUET:
The scent a wine gives off after it is poured. Bouquet results from aging, both in the tank and in the bottle.

BURGER:
A white wine grape, formerly very popular in the Valley as the basis for Chablis. Now not very popular and rapidly being replaced.

CAP:
The mass of grape skins, pulp, and seeds that floats over the fermenting grape juice. (Red wine only.)

CABERNET FRANC:
A red wine grape, popular in France as a blending agent, but not generally grown in the Napa Valley.

CABERNET SAUVIGNON:
A red wine grape, originally the great grape of the Bordeaux region. Although a sparse bearer it is popularly conceded to yield the greatest red wine of the Napa Valley.

CELLARMAN:
A worker in a winery, who transfers wine, scrubs fermenting tanks, etc.

CENTRIFUGE:
A machine which uses the principle of centrifugal force to clear particulate matter from wine. It operates on the same principle as the old cream-separator.

CHABLIS:
A generic name for wine made from almost any white grape. Named after the Chablis region in France.

CHAMPAGNE:
In the United States, just about any naturally fermented sparkling wine. In France, only those sparkling wines that originate in the district of Champagne. Thus, American champagne wines, even very good ones, may not be sold in France as "champagne."

CHARMAT PROCESS:
A method of making champagne whereby the wine is fermented in a large container and bottled under pressure without fermentation taking place in the bottle.

CHARDONNAY:
Also sometimes called Pinot Chardonnay. A noble white grape originally from Burgundy, from which a big, full white wine is made.

COASTAL ZONE:
One of the five climactic zones into which grape growing areas are divided. The Coastal Zone is of medium warmth.

CONTINUOUS PRESS:
A wine press in which the grape pulp is fed in and the press wine and pomace extracted continuously.

CRUSH:
The time during which the grapes are harvested and turned into wine.

CRUSHING:
The process whereby the grapes are broken open and juice is liberated.

DEGREES BALLING:
A scale method of measuring sugar content in grape juice. Usually marked °B. Also called Brix.

ESTATE BOTTLING:
Designation given a wine which is totally produced on the winery's property. Thus, the grapes are grown in the winery's vineyards, and all the operations from crushing to bottling are performed in the winery's cellars.

FALLING BRIGHT:
A spontaneous clearing of suspended material from wine without outside help.

FERMENTOR:
Any container which is used to ferment grape juice into wine. Formerly made of wood or concrete, they are now made mostly of glass or stainless steel.

FINING:
The process of clearing the wine of suspended material.

FLORA:
A hybrid grape, developed at University of California Davis. Has a sweet taste similar to the Traminer.

FREE RUN:
The juice that results from the first crushing of the grapes, without pressing.

FRENCH COLOMBARD:
An aromatic white wine grape, or the wine made from it. Almost always used as a blending grape in France, it is increasingly popular in the Napa Valley as a varietal.

GAMAY:
A red wine grape, originally from the Beaujolais region in France, now grown extensively in the Napa Valley. It produces a fruity, light red wine, best drunk when young.

GENERIC (wines):
A wine named after the region in which it originated, or which has the general characteristics of such a wine.

GOLDEN CHASSELAS:
A heavy-bearing white wine grape once very popular in the Valley, but now being largely replaced. Also called "Palomino."

GONDOLA:
A wheeled open-topped horizontal tank that is used to collect grapes.

GREEN HUNGARIAN:
A white wine grape, often made into a varietal in the Napa Valley. Origin unknown, in spite of the name.

JUG WINE:
Wine of no particular breed or standing, which is usually sold in quantity. (Jugs.)

MARITIME ZONE:
One of the five climactic zones in which grape growing areas are divided. This one is the coolest.

MEDOC:
Part of the Bordeaux region. One of the great wine-grape growing regions of France.

MERLOT:
A red wine grape, not usually considered noble, of considerable merit because it is usually blended with Cabernet Sauvignon to achieve the best red wines of Bordeaux.

METHODE CHAMPENOISE:
The original French method of making champagne wherein a second fermentation is induced in the bottle, with the carbon dioxide dissolved into the bottled wine.

MICRO CLIMATE:
A special set of growing conditions, usually confined to a small area. This could be induced by soil content, availability of water, or by geographical features of the site.

MISSION GRAPE:
A heavy-bearing, somewhat sweet grape, probably of Mexican or Spanish origin, which was first planted in California by the early Franciscan Missionaries.

MOSCATO CANELLI:
A very sweet white wine grape of the muscat family; it makes a very sweet, luscious wine.

MUST:
The pulped grapes, as they come out of the crusher and into the fermenting tank.

NOBLE GRAPES:
Those varieties of grapes that yield the best wines, such as Cabernet, Sauvignon, Pinot Noir, Pinot Chardonnay. Usually they are hard to grow, yield sparsely, and like all good things, are achieved only with some difficulty.

NOSE:
The particular aromatic odor that is peculiar to any one wine.

OIDIUM:
A grape disease characterized by a powdery film of spores that attacks and mildews grapes.

PETITE SIRRAH:
A red wine grape, originally from France, which is made into a varietal wine in the Napa Valley.

PHYLLOXERA:
A vine disease caused by a tiny underground louse that eats European rootstock.

PINOT NOIR:
A red wine grape, originally from Burgundy, which in the Southern Napa Valley yields an excellent varietal wine. Also, the wine made from this grape.

PINOT ST. GEORGE:
A red wine grape. Mostly grown in the hillside vineyards of the Napa Valley. Also the wine made from this grape.

POMACE:
The residue remaining after wine has been pressed from the must.

PRESSING:
The process by which wine is extracted from fermented must. Done by squeezing the fermented, pulped grapes.

RACKING:
The drawing off of wine, above the sediment. Done several times during the aging process to achieve maximum clarity.

RED WINE:
Wine produced from black (really dark blue) skinned grapes, that has acquired the pigmentation of its parent.

REFRACTOMETER:
An optical instrument that measures sugar content in grape juice by means of optical refraction.

RHEINGAU:
A major grape-producing area in Germany bordering on the river Rhine.

ROSE WINE:
Wine made from red grapes, which has a light rose color, acquired by only short contact with the skins.

SET:
The fertilization of grape flowers that will grow into grapes.

SUCKERS:
Non-productive canes.

TARTRATES:
Salts of tartaric acid, that accumulate in an aging tank, and must be regularly removed.

TRAMINER:
A white wine grape, originally from Alsace. In the Napa Valley it yields a light, fruity, slightly sweet wine.

VARIETALS (wines):
A wine named after the grape from which it is made.

VINIFERA:
A family of grapes whose characteristics lend themselves to making good wine. All Napa Valley grapes are of the Vinifera family.

VINTAGE DATING:
The classification of a wine according to the year in which it was fermented.

WHITE RIESLING:
A white wine grape, originally of German origin, source of the popular Johannisberg Riesling wine. Also "Riesling," the wine made from that grape.

WHITE WINE:
Wine produced from (usually) white or yellow grapes and fermented out of contact with the skins. Theoretically, white wine can be made from red grapes by fermenting it out of contact with the skins, but why bother?

WINE:
An alcoholic beverage made from the fermented juice of the grape. Thus, beverages made from fruits, berries, etc., while they are undeniably alcoholic beverages are not, strictly speaking, wine.

WINE-THIEF:
A hollow glass tube open at both ends. With one end plugged by a finger, after the tube has been inserted in the wine-barrel, it easily transfers wine from the barrel to the taster's glass.

ZINFANDEL:
A red wine grape, or the wine made from it. Originally imported into California by Count Agoston Haraszthy.

PHOTO DATA

Professional photographers have long known that there is no one camera that will always be the best suited for a particular picture when the assignment entails a variety of situations. Selection of the photographic equipment used to do this book; therefore, became a matter of compromise; the choice would inevitably boil down to that equipment which would do the best overall job, even though some other size could admittedly be better for any one specific picture. It was, therefore, almost inevitable that I should again turn to the 35 mm, since this equipment has demonstrated a versatility unmatched by any other format.

The toughness, portability, wide variety of lenses and excellence of its optics made the Nikon system a logical choice, although it must be admitted that a camera that has triumphantly weathered a year in the tall timber, during the shooting of *Timber Country,* became in two weeks, my first casualty. A fall from a thirty foot high vantage point, with a tripod attached, to a very hard concrete floor reduced a metering head to a mass of high-priced optical junk, although the body survived intact and completed the assignment without a hitch.

It is high tribute to the quality built into these instruments that in spite of the all pervasive dust, moisture, sticky grape-juice and the inevitable beating that a camera in hard professional use gets, they are all today in perfect working order.

Four Nikon FTN bodies, and one Nikkormat were used to make the pictures in this book. Unless otherwise noted, all exposures were on Kodachrome II film, rated at ASA 25. Lenses used, all Nikkors, in order of focal length were:

20 mm	f 3.5	55 mm	f 1.2
28 mm	f 3.5	85 mm	f 1.8
35 mm	f 2	105 mm	f 2.5
35 mm	f 2.8 P.C.	135 mm	f 3.5
50 mm	f 1.4	200 mm	f 4.0
50 mm	f 2	300 mm	f 4.5
55 mm	f 3.5 Macro		

All lenses, unless noted otherwise, were capped with skylight filters. Two flash units were used; a small pocket Ultrablitz and a 200 watt-second Matador, with extension heads, that is a wonderfully versatile and powerful unit.

Earl Roberge
American Society of Magazine Photographers

Page				
Cover	1/250 @ f 4.5	300 mm	Tripod	
V	1/125 @ f 5.6	50 mm	f 1.4	
VIII-IX	1/60 @ f 8	50 mm	f 2	
X	1/250 @ f 4	105 mm		
XI	1/60 @ f 4	50 mm		
XII-XIII	1/125 @ f 4	105 mm	f 1.4 Deep Shade	
XIV-XV	1/125 @ f 5.6	28 mm		
XVI	1/250 @ f 4	50 mm	f 1.4 Kodachrome X	
XVII	1/250 @ f 5.6	135 mm		
XVIII	1/8 @ f 16	28 mm	Tripod	
22	1/125 @ f 4	28 mm	Pola Screen	
23	1/15 @ f 5.6	55 mm	Macro, Tripod, with fill in flash held six feet from cluster	
24-25	1/4 @ f 5.6	300 mm	Tripod	
26	1/60 @ f 8	35 mm	P.C. Tripod	
27	1/60 @ f 5.6	50 mm	f 2	
28-29	1/4 @ f 16	28 mm	Pola Screen, Tripod	
30	1/125 @ f 4	55 mm	Macro	
31	1/30 @ f 16	50 mm	f 1.4	
32	1/125 @ f 2.5	105 mm		
33	1/60 @ f 8	35 mm	PC Pola Screen Kodachrome X	

34	1/30 @ f 8	55 mm	Macro	
35	1/125 @ f 5.6	35 mm	f 2	
36	1/250 @ f 5.6	105 mm		
37	1/30 @ f 4	85 mm		
38	1 Sec. @ f 4	105 mm	Almost dark, Tripod	
39	1/125 @ f 2	35 mm	f 2	
40-41	1/60 @ f 5.6	35 mm	f 2	
42	1/250 @ f 8	85 mm	Kodachrome X	
43	1/250 @ f 4	105 mm		
44-45	1/250 @ f 8	35 mm	f 2, Kodachrome X	
46	1/250 @ f 5.6	50 mm	f 2	
47	1 Sec. @ f 4	28 mm	Type A Kodachrome, Tripod	
48	1/8 Sec. @ f 4	55 mm	Macro, Very dark	
49	1/60 @ f 5.6	35 mm	f 2	
50	1/60 @ f 5.6	85 mm	Pola Screen, Tripod	
51	1/30 @ f 4	35 mm	Cloudy and dark	
52	1/125 @ f 8	50 mm	f 1.4	
53	1/15 @ f 5.6	105 mm	Tripod	
54	1/250 @ f 5.6	50 mm	f 2	
55	1/125 @ f 8	50 mm	f 1.4	
56-57	1/125 @ f 8	50 mm	f 1.4	
58	1/125 @ f 8	35 mm	f 2, Kodachrome X	
59	1/125 @ f 5.6	28 mm		
60-61	1/15 @ f 8	20 mm	Pola Screen, Tripod	
62	8 Sec. @ f 4	28 mm	Kodachrome Type A, Tripod	
63	30 Sec. @ f 4	28 mm	Kodachrome Type A, Tripod	
64	1/250 @ f 5.6	50 mm	f 1.4	
65	2 Min. @ f 8	28 mm	Type A Kodachrome, Tripod	
66	1/15 @ f 1.4	50 mm	f 1.4, Fluorescent Filter	
67	1/125 @ f 5.6	50 mm	f 2	
68	1/60 @ f 8	50 mm	f 1.4	
69	2 Min. @ f 8	35 mm	P.C., Type A Kodachrome, Tripod	
70	1/125 @ f 5.6	35 mm	f 2 (with insufficient flash)	
71	1/250 @ f 5.6	50 mm	f 1.4	
72-73	45 Min. @ f 11	20 mm	Tripod	

Because these are only 15 watt bulbs and the exposure was extremely long, I used Kodachrome II rather than Kodachrome Type A, which has a tendency to shift color under very long exposures.

74	1/250 @ f 4	105 mm		
75	1/60 @ f 2.8	50 mm	f 1.4	
76-77	1/60 @ f 11	35 mm	f 2	
78	1/30 @ f 4	35 mm	f 2.8	
79	1/250 @ f 5.6	50 mm	f 2	
80	1/250 @ f 5.6	135 mm		
81	1/60 @ f 8	85 mm	Multiple (2) flash	
82	1/15 @ f 2.8	35 mm	f 2 (Tripod), Kodachrome Type A	
83	45 Sec. @ f 8	28 mm	Kodachrome Type A, Tripod	
84	1/125 @ f 5.6	50 mm	Early morning	
85	1/8 @ f 4	28 mm	Handheld!	
86	1 Sec. @ f 8	35 mm	P.C. Fluorescent filter, Tripod	
87	1/30 @ f 5.6	35 mm	P.C. Polascreen	
88-89	1/250 @ f 5.6	50 mm	f 2	
90	1/60 @ f 8	105 mm	Multiple flash (3 heads) in daylight	
91	1/125 @ f 5.6	35 mm	f 2, Polascreen	

Page	Exposure	Lens	Notes
92-93	1/60 @ f 8	35 mm	f 2 with 200 watt sec. flash fill
94	1 Sec. @ f 11	200 mm	Tripod
95	1/30 @ f 16	28 mm	
96	15 Sec. @ f 8	28 mm	Fluorescent filter and Tripod
97	1/250 @ f 5.6	300 mm	
98	1/4 @ f 4	28 mm	
99	10 Sec. @ f 8	20 mm	Tripod
100	1/60 @ f 4	35 mm	f x, Kodachrome X
101	15 Sec. @ f 5.6	28 mm	Tripod
102	1/125 @ f 5.6	50 mm	f 2, Early morning
103	1/15 @ f 16	28 mm	Tripod
104-105	1/250 @ f 4	50 mm	f 2
106	1/15 @ f 2.8	50 mm	f 1.4
107	1/60 @ f 8	50 mm	f 1.4, Kodachrome X, Raining
108-109	1/15 @ f 11	55 mm	Macro, Pola Screen
110	1/15 @ f 5.6	105 mm	Kodachrome A, modeling lamps from Honeywell Strobonars used as light source. Tripod.
111	1/60 @ f 5.6	28 mm	Raining
112	1/250 @ f 5.6	50 mm	f 2, From wind tower
113	1/60 @ f 5.6	35 mm	P.C., Tripod
114	1/30 @ f 4	105 mm	lighted by 3-Victor Halogen lights
115	1/60 @ f 5.6	200 mm	The rim light comes from a flash unit positioned 10 feet to one side and behind Bro. Tim. Triggered using a 40 ft. cord.
116	1/250 @ f 5.6	50 mm	f 2
117	1/125 @ f 8	50 mm	f 1.4
118	1/15 @ f 11	28 mm	Lens lighted by three Victor Halogen lamp units. Tripod
119	30 Sec. @ f 5.6	50 mm	f 2, Kodachrome Type A, Tripod
120-121	1/60 @ f 11	35 mm	f 2
122	1/125 @ f 4	105 mm	Cloudy
123	8 Sec. @ f 8	35 mm	f 2, Type A Kodachrome, Tripod
124-125	1/30 @ f 4	20 mm	and Polascreen Taken while balancing (nervously) on top of the thirty-foot arch at the entrance to Greystone.
126	1/60 @ f 5.6	35 mm	f 2, Shooting against the light
127	1/60 @ f 5.6	50 mm	f 1.4
128	1/4 @ f 8	55 mm	with weak fill in flash, Macro, Tripod
129	1/30 @ f 8	55 mm	Macro
130	1/125 @ f 5.6	28 mm	
131	1/60 @ f 8	85 mm	with fill in flash
132	1/30 @ f 4	35 mm	f 2
133	15 Sec. @ f 11	20 mm	Tripod
134	1/125 @ f 5.6	50 mm	f 1.4
135	8 Sec. @ f 8	28 mm	Tripod
136-137	1/4 @ f 1.4	50 mm	f 1.4, Haldheld, almost dark
138	1/250 @ f 5.6	50 mm	f 2
139	1/60 @ f 5.6	50 mm	f 1.4
140-141	1/125 @ f 8	50 mm	f 1.4
142	1/4 @ f 2.8	50 mm	f 1.4, Tripod
143	10 Sec. @ f 8	28 mm	Tripod
144	1/30 @ f 11	50 mm	f 1.4
145	10 Min. @ f 11	20 mm	Tripod, Kodachrome A
146	1/30 @ f 4	35 mm	P.C. Tripod
147	1/60 @ f 4	35 mm	P.C. Polascreen
148	1/60 @ f 11	85 mm	Fill in flash
149	1/125 @ f 8	105 mm	
150	1/125 @ f 8	55 mm	f 1.2
151	1/60 @ f 8	105 mm	
152-153	1 Sec. @ f 5.6	20 mm	Tripod
154	1/15 @ f 8	35 mm	f 2
155	1/125 @ f 5.6	50 mm	f 1.4
156	1/250 @ f 5.6	50 mm	f 1.4
157	1/60 @ f 8	28 mm	Flash, bounced off curved surface at the right of the picture
158	1/125 @ f 4	50 mm	f 1.4 early morning
159	1/60 @ f 4	55 mm	f 1.2
160	1/30 @ f 4	50 mm	f 2
161	1/250 @ f 5.6	85 mm	
162	1/250 @ f 5.6	300 mm	
163	1/30 @ f 8	55 mm	Macro
164	1/250 @ f 5.6	200 mm	from the top of a tree as vantage point
165	1/500 @ f 4	200 mm	
166	1/30 @ f 4	50 mm	f 1.4
167	1/60 @ f 8	135 mm	
168-169	45 Sec. @ f 4	35 mm	f 2, Light supplied by smudge pots only, at early dawn. Tripod
170	1/125 @ f 4	55 mm	Macro
171	1/30 @ f 5.6	50 mm	f 1.4
172	1 Sec. @ f 4	55 mm	f 1.2, Type A, Tripod
173	1 Sec. @ f 11	55 mm	Macro, Tripod
174	1/60 @ f 5.6	55 mm	Macro
175	1/125 @ f 5.6	135 mm	
176	1/125 @ f 4	55 mm	Macro
177	1/60 @ f 8	105 mm	With weak fill in flash. Because of slow shutter speed necessitated by flash synchronization, foot movement was watched critically
178	1/125 @ f 5.6	50 mm	f 1.4
179	1/60 @ f 5.6	55 mm	Macro
180	1/250 @ f 4	85 mm	
181	1/60 @ f 11	35 mm	f 2, with 3 synchronized flash heads; one aimed at face, one level with the wine surface and one at 45° angle from the camera and 8' above the vat
182	1 Sec. @ f 2.8	55 mm	f 1.2, with fluorescent filter, Tripod
183	1/60 @ f 4	105 mm	
184-185	1/15 @ f 11	55 mm	With camera rested on edge of crusher, Macro and lots of patience.
186	1/250 @ f 5.6	300 mm	across swimming pool
187	1/500 @ f 4	50 mm	f 2
188	1/60 @ f 16	50 mm	f 2, Two flash heads
189	1 Sec. @ f 4	35 mm	f 2, Tripod
190	1/60 @ f 4	50 mm	f 1.4, Kodachrome X, Late afternoon
191	1/125 @ f 4	28 mm	
192	1/60 @ f 2.5	105 mm	
193	1/15 @ f 4	105 mm	
194	1/60 @ f 8	85 mm	with fill in flash
195	1/60 @ f 5.6	55 mm	Macro
196	1/125 @ f 5.6	300 mm	
197	1/60 @ f 8	55 mm	Macro
198	1/125 @ f 5.6	105 mm	
199	1/60 @ f 11	105 mm	Electronic flash— 3 Units
200-201	1/125 @ f 5.6	35 mm	f 2
202	1/250 @ f 4.5	300 mm	Pola Screen
203	1/60 @ f 5.6	35 mm	Pola Screen